Harry Potter™

HERMIONE GRANGER™

CINEMATIC GUIDE

SCHOLASTIC INC.

Contents

Film Beginnings

Hermione Granger grew up in a Muggle family that was proud when she got her letter from Hogwarts. From the moment she boarded the Hogwarts Express as a first year, she showed a talent for magic and spellwork.

In the first Harry Potter film, Hermione meets Harry and Ron on the Hogwarts Express, a train that brings students from King's Cross station in London to Hogwarts castle at the start of each school year.

HOGWARTS EXPRESS

"You're Harry Potter, aren't you?
I know all about you, of course."

—HERMIONE GRANGER, *HARRY POTTER*
AND THE SORCERER'S STONE FILM

Hermione makes quite an impression when she enters Ron and Harry's train compartment.

Hermione casts a spell to fix Harry's broken glasses with the words "Oculus Reparo."

Hermione and all the other first-year students disembark from the train and take boats across the lake to get to Hogwarts castle.

Hogwarts School of Witchcraft and Wizardry becomes a second home to Hermione. Over her six years at Hogwarts, she earns a reputation both for her dazzling intelligence and eagerness to help others.

Life at Hogwarts

After their arrival at Hogwarts, it's time to get sorted. Each student is placed into one of the four houses: Gryffindor, Hufflepuff, Ravenclaw, or Slytherin.

Hermione is clever enough to be sorted into Ravenclaw, but, as she hoped, she's placed in Gryffindor.

Harry and Ron are also sorted into Gryffindor.

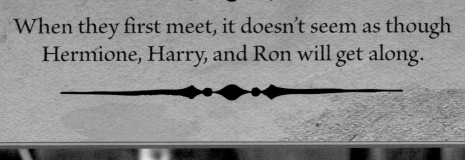

When they first meet, it doesn't seem as though Hermione, Harry, and Ron will get along.

"*Stop, stop, stop! You're going to take someone's eye out. Besides, you're saying it wrong. It's Leviosa not Leviosa.*"

—HERMIONE GRANGER, HARRY POTTER
AND THE SORCERER'S STONE FILM

A dangerous event forges the start of Hermione, Harry, and Ron's extraordinary friendship.

Hermione is in the bathroom when a giant troll wanders in! Harry and Ron hear a troll is on the loose and go looking for Hermione to warn her.

Harry and Ron defeat the troll just in time. When the teachers appear and see that Harry and Ron have broken the rules by fighting the troll, Hermione takes the blame.

Hermione quickly proves herself
to be a clever and dedicated student by
excelling in all of her subjects.

"*Do you take pride in being an insufferable know-it-all? Five points from Gryffindor!*"

—Professor Snape to Hermione,
*Harry Potter and the
Prisoner of Azkaban* film

Hermione's teachers take notice of her intelligence and love of learning.

"Well, well, well, Hermione, you really are the brightest witch of your age I've ever met."

—PROFESSOR LUPIN, HARRY POTTER AND THE PRISONER OF AZKABAN FILM

"They've yet to think of a spell that our Hermione can't do."

—RUBEUS HAGRID, HARRY POTTER AND THE CHAMBER OF SECRETS FILM

But not all classes are easy for Hermione. In her third year, Hermione discovers the one Hogwarts subject she doesn't care for: Divination, the art of divining the future. Hermione prefers logical subjects without so much guesswork.

"*From the first moment you stepped foot in my class, I sensed that you did not possess the proper spirit for the noble art of Divination.*"

—PROFESSOR TRELAWNEY, *HARRY POTTER AND THE PRISONER OF AZKABAN* FILM

Hermione occasionally takes a break from her studies to have fun. She becomes the talk of Hogwarts when she attends the Yule Ball with famous Quidditch player Viktor Krum from Durmstrang.

Ron is jealous that Hermione goes to the Yule Ball with Viktor instead of with him.

"*Next time there's a ball, pluck up the courage to ask me before somebody else does, and not as a last resort!*"

—HERMIONE GRANGER, *HARRY POTTER AND THE GOBLET OF FIRE* FILM

Hermione starts off her time at Hogwarts as a stickler for the rules. However, as she gets older, she finds the value in breaking them occasionally.

"*Now if you two don't mind, I'm going to bed before either of you come up with another clever idea to get us killed—or worse, expelled.*"

—HERMIONE GRANGER, *HARRY POTTER AND THE SORCERER'S STONE* FILM

> *"It's sort of exciting, isn't it?*
> *Breaking the rules."*
>
> — HERMIONE, HARRY POTTER AND
> THE ORDER OF THE PHOENIX FILM

Family, Friends, and Foes

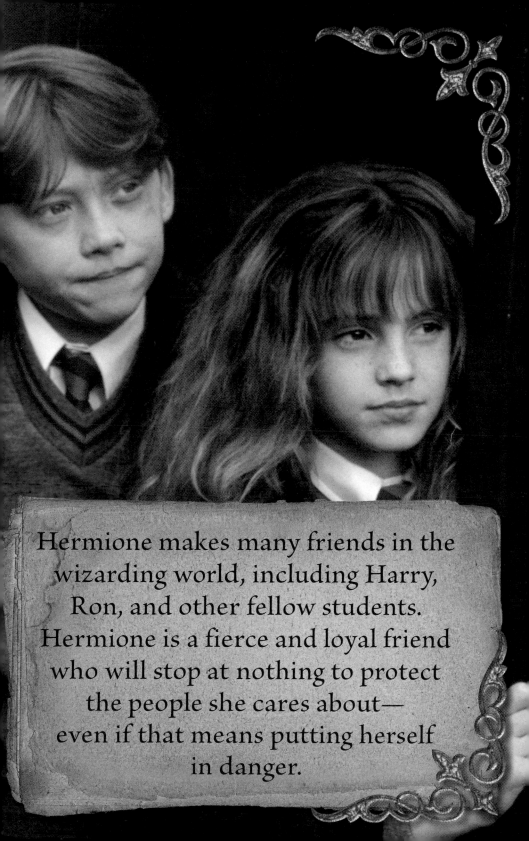

Hermione makes many friends in the
wizarding world, including Harry,
Ron, and other fellow students.
Hermione is a fierce and loyal friend
who will stop at nothing to protect
the people she cares about—
even if that means putting herself
in danger.

Hermione, just like Harry's mother, was born to Muggle parents.

Hermione comes from an ordinary and loving family.

Hermione: "My parents are dentists. They tend to people's teeth."

Professor Slughorn: "Fascinating, and is that considered a dangerous profession?"

—Harry Potter and the Half-Blood Prince film

Hermione is often teased about having non-magical parents, especially by Draco Malfoy, who calls her a "Mudblood."

"There are some wizards—like the Malfoy family—who think they're better than everyone else because they're what people call pureblood."

—Rubeus Hagrid, *Harry Potter and the Chamber of Secrets* film

Draco and his friends

Hermione's parents are proud she's a witch. However, she wipes their memories to keep them out of danger from Lord Voldemort's Death Eaters.

"Obliviate."

—Hermione Granger,
*Harry Potter and the
Deathly Hallows –
Part 1* film

Hermione comforts her friends when they are upset.

In Defense Against the Dark Arts class, Mad-Eye Moody demonstrates the Cruciatus Curse, a torture spell that was used on Neville Longbottom's parents. After class, Hermione comforts Neville.

Hermione gives Harry a pep talk before he competes in the Triwizard Tournament.

Hermione: "The key is to concentrate. After that you just have to~"

Harry: "Battle a dragon."

—HARRY POTTER AND THE GOBLET OF FIRE FILM

In their sixth year, Hermione stays by Ron's hospital bedside after
he accidentally drinks poison meant for Professor Dumbledore and
ends up in the hospital wing.

When Hermione thinks that Sirius Black, an escapee from Azkaban prison, wants to hurt Harry, she puts herself in harm's way to protect him from danger.

"If you want to kill Harry, you'll have to kill us, too."

HERMIONE GRANGER, *HARRY POTTER AND THE PRISONER OF AZKABAN* FILM

Hermione refuses to let Harry search for Lord Voldemort's hidden Horcruxes on his own. Hermione knows she needs to be by her friend's side on such a dangerous mission.

"You don't really think you're going to be able to find all those Horcruxes by yourself, do you? You need us."

—HERMIONE GRANGER, *HARRY POTTER AND THE HALF-BLOOD PRINCE* FILM

Hermione refuses to divulge any secrets about their Horcrux hunt—even under torture by Bellatrix Lestrange, a vicious Death Eater.

Hermione is protective of the people she cares about most. She stands up for Hagrid and Buckbeak when Draco makes light of the Hippogriff's impending execution.

"You foul, loathsome, evil little cockroach!"

—Hermione Granger, Harry Potter
and the Prisoner of Azkaban film

Cleverest Moments

Hermione is known at Hogwarts as the brightest witch of her age. On her many adventures with Harry and Ron, it is often thanks to Hermione's educated mind, grasp of logic, and quick thinking that the trio safely escapes and succeeds.

Hermione often saves the day by applying what she has learned in class to sticky situations.

Hermione is the one who realizes that Hagrid's three-headed dog, Fluffy, is standing on top of the trapdoor guarding the Sorcerer's Stone.

Hermione uses her knowledge of Herbology, especially dangerous plants, to help Harry find the Sorcerer's Stone hidden in Hogwarts castle.

"Devil's Snare, Devil's Snare . . . 'It's deadly fun . . . but will sulk in the sun!' That's it!"

—HERMIONE GRANGER, *HARRY POTTER AND THE SORCERER'S STONE* FILM

In their second year, Professor Lockhart frees a cage full of Cornish pixies in Defense Against the Dark Arts class.

Hermione is the only one who knows the spell that can stop the mischievous little creatures.

"Immobulus!"

— HERMIONE GRANGER, HARRY POTTER
AND THE CHAMBER OF SECRETS FILM

Over the years, Hermione becomes an expert at brewing Polyjuice Potion, which allows the user to take on another person's appearance.

Hermione uses Polyjuice Potion to impersonate Death Eater
Bellatrix Lestrange.

She also uses it to sneak into the Ministry of Magic
with Harry and Ron.

Through research at the library, Hermione discovers that the mysterious beast in the Chamber of Secrets is a Basilisk, also known as the King of Serpents.

Anyone who looks a Basilisk *directly* in the eye will perish.

Hermione sees the Basilisk *indirectly* in a mirror. She survives, but is Petrified—literally turned to stone.

Before being Petrified, Hermione left a clue about the Basilisk for Harry and Ron to find.

Thanks to Hermione, Harry is able to defeat the Basilisk and save Hogwarts from its terror and destruction.

Hermione uses a Time-Turner to go back in time to save Hagrid's Hippogriff, Buckbeak, and Harry's godfather, Sirius Black.

Hermione and Harry watch as past events unfold.

While on the run with Harry and Ron, Hermione puts an Undetectable Extension Charm on her small, purple bag. That way Hermione can be prepared for any situation.

The charm allows the inside of the bag to expand to fit whatever she needs to carry, while appearing to be its original size on the outside.

She keeps a magical tent in the bag that comes in very handy while they are hunting for Horcruxes.

When Ron gets Splinched after Disapparating from the Ministry, Hermione uses the Essence of Dittany she keeps in her bag to heal his wounds.

When Harry, Ron, and Hermione break into Gringotts in disguise to find a Horcrux, their cover is blown and Hermione must find a way to get them out alive.

Hermione: "Who's got an idea?"

Ron: "You're the brilliant one."

Hermione: "I've got something, but it's mad!"

—HARRY POTTER AND THE
DEATHLY HALLOWS – PART 2 FILM

Hermione daringly jumps onto the fire-breathing dragon that guards the Gringotts' vaults. It bursts through the roof, soaring through the sky with Hermione, Ron, and Harry holding on for their lives.

Fighting Dark Forces

Hermione's determination and pluck, combined with her brilliance at spells, make her one of Harry Potter's strongest allies. She fights by his side at a number of important battles.

In her fifth year, Hermione has the idea to start the secret group Dumbledore's Army to teach her fellow students how to defend themselves against Dark magic.

Hermione convinces Harry to teach their classmates defensive magic.

"We've got to be able to defend ourselves. And if Umbridge refuses to teach us how, we need someone who will."

—HERMIONE GRANGER, *HARRY POTTER AND THE ORDER OF THE PHOENIX* FILM

During a DA session, students learn to produce a Patronus, a spell that wards off Dementors.

Members of Dumbledore's Army have their skills put to the test.

When a group of Snatchers discovers Hermione, Harry, and Ron's hiding place in the woods, Hermione thinks fast and figures out a way to buy them time to disguise who they truly are.

Hermione uses a spell to make Harry's face swell, making it difficult for the Snatchers to recognize him.

The Snatchers take them to Malfoy Manor in the hope that Draco will be able to identify his former classmates.

Hermione plays a crucial part in the final battle of Hogwarts, and Lord Voldemort's ultimate downfall.

Hermione and Ron go into the Chamber of Secrets in search of a Basilisk fang that will destroy the lost diadem of Ravenclaw, a Horcrux.

Hermione and Ron are so relieved to be alive they finally admit their true feelings for each other and kiss.

"We wouldn't last two days
without her."

—RON WEASLEY, HARRY POTTER AND
THE DEATHLY HALLOWS – PART 2 FILM

About the Book

The time is 1775, when early thunder rumbled over Massachusetts, thunder before the coming storm of the Revolutionary War. The place is Salem—for a brief strategic period the capital of the colony. The hero is fourteen-year-old Daniel West—a boy with a decision to make.

Though he was a dedicated Tory, Daniel hated the growing violence of the Whig-Tory conflict which split Salem and its people. He despised the rowdy Liberty Boys creeping up to Tory porches with their "Liberty gifts"—buckets of garbage.

Yet as the year went by, the events that were shaping a new nation reached relentlessly into every corner of Daniel's life. England disappointed him. His father disappointed him. Then, on a night when Salem went wild, Daniel disappointed himself.

Daniel's struggle to find his place, a stand he could take proudly, is resolved in a confrontation between the British troops and the townspeople—a true incident that nearly started the war. This is the first time in children's fiction that the events of this decisive year in Salem have been chronicled in such detail. The result is a real and engrossing novel of a boy's year of decision which has special significance for today.

EARLY
THUNDER

by Jean Fritz

Illustrated by Lynd Ward

Coward, McCann & Geoghegan New York

Seventh Impression

SBN: GB 698-20036-5

Library of Congress Catalog Card Number: 67-24217

Printed in the United States of America

For Sabra

EARLY THUNDER

Chapter One

DANIEL WEST couldn't sleep and he couldn't go outside unless he felt like courting trouble, so what he did was to get up, pull the blankets off his bed, wrap himself up in them, and then settle down in a chair by his bedroom window. At least he'd look out. If the Liberty Boys were up to anything, he'd see it. And while he was looking, he'd see if he could find one thing that was right in the world.

He'd start with the weather. Bad. The old folks said the winter of 1773 to 1774 was one of the worst in memory, and even now, in the middle of March, there were chunks of ice knocking about the harbor. He didn't have to be outside to feel the cold; he could see it in the stiff way the trees held themselves, creaking when the wind moved them as if they had the rheumatism.

Daniel pulled the blankets around him more closely and moved from the weather to the world at large. He couldn't see much of it from his window and he had a hard time picturing it—a round ball wrapped up in forests and rivers and houses and people. When he tried to picture it, it came out not round but shaped like a triangle, an isosceles triangle. Boston and Salem were at two points of the triangle and London was at the third. London was there because that's where the king was and Lord North who started the tea tax, Boston because it had defied the tax and dumped the tea in the harbor, and Salem because Salem was Here. Salem was where Daniel lived and where the folks he knew were awaiting the Punishment. Sometime in spring the news could come—from London to Boston, and from there riders would go out to neighboring towns because whatever England did about the Tea Party would affect the province, the whole country, the future of everyone.

Some people didn't think the Punishment would amount to much. Lord North would see that there were things Americans wouldn't stand for and he'd repeal the tax. Then everyone would be friends again—

the Whigs, or Patriots as they called themselves, who believed the country should defy any government that threatened its rights, and the Tories, men like Dr. West, Daniel's father, who believed a country should submit to unjust laws until they could be properly changed.

But there were others who just shook their heads. We'd gone too far, they said. We were in for it now.

Meanwhile there were the Liberty Boys, the rowdy branch of the Patriot side. Daniel sighed, knotting his hands into fists under the blankets. They'd be on the prowl tonight—the eve of the anniversary of the repeal of the stamp tax. Any little cause for celebration and they were out, delivering their Liberty Gifts. A little pile of garbage on the steps of one Tory house, a shovelful of manure of the steps of another. Fortunately, nothing had ever been left at Dr. West's. Daniel guessed folks still felt sorry for his father, but more than once Daniel's best friend, Beckett Foote, had found rotten eggs or some sort of unsavory mess on his doormat.

Daniel studied the scene out the window. The town seemed peaceful enough now, he decided. There wasn't a sign of life. Too peaceful maybe. And dark. Suddenly Daniel wished he'd see a candle someplace, but no matter what direction he looked, there wasn't a single window that was lighted. He wished he'd see Jeremy Packer, the night watchman, but it was too early for Jeremy. Up to this time he hadn't thought much about the fact that he was alone in the house. His father was in Boston again and Sarah, his eight-

11

year-old sister, was spending the night at the Widow Ray's. Of course, he wasn't quite alone. There was still Hannah, the cook, but she was asleep in the downstairs bedroom and anyone who slept as soundly as Hannah wasn't much company.

Daniel shivered. If only there'd be an animal, he thought, to cross the street! And this, of course, gave Daniel another point to add to his list of things that had gone wrong with the world. Because there weren't any animals in Salem. At least there were no dogs or cats, nor had there been since the ordinance last fall that they had to be killed. Cats and dogs were said to carry smallpox. And in addition to everything else, this winter would be remembered in Salem as the Winter of the Smallpox. Twenty people had died in the Pest House; hundreds had gone to the new hospital to be inoculated and some of them had contracted the disease in the process. Even now Judge Ropes, who lived across from Beckett, was seriously sick in his own home from an inoculation that had gone wrong.

Daniel turned from the window. He couldn't bear to look out at the dark, lonely town any longer. He decided to go down to the kitchen and see if he could stir up some fire and some food. Besides, in narrowing down his grievances with the world, he was coming pretty close to his own family and Daniel couldn't think about that. He'd got to the point he could accept the changes the winter had made but he couldn't dwell on them. He could tell folks that his mother had died in December after giving birth to his brother, Jonathon, but as soon as he'd said that, he'd go on quickly

12

and explain that Jonathon was being cared for by Tillie Packer, Jeremy's wife. The thought of Tillie and Jonathon together in the snug house near the North River was a comfort.

Daniel squatted down before the kitchen hearth, poked at the embers until they looked ready to be fed, then gave them some kindling and a couple of logs. Then he put a lighted candle on the window ledge. If Jeremy Packer saw a light when he came by on his rounds, he might stop in for a warm-up by the fire.

He'd hardly set the candle down when there was a knock at the back door. Daniel stepped back from the candle, although, of course, whoever it was had already seen him. It was too late for callers, too early for Jeremy. The knock came again—an urgent knock followed by a laugh. Daniel backed up toward the fireplace and reached for the poker. Then a voice spoke in a muffled whisper as though someone were holding his mouth close to the door.

"Open up," the voice said, "in the name of the law." There was another laugh. "In the name of the king, in the name of heaven, in the name of anything you will, only it's bitter cold out here, Daniel West."

It was Beckett. Daniel grinned, put the poker back and unlatched the door.

"I thought it was one of our liberty friends," he said as Beckett strode toward the fire, holding his hands out to the warmth. He had obviously been in bed because his clothes were put on carelessly and under his greatcoat his shirt was buttoned askew.

"What's the matter?" Daniel asked.

13

Beckett tossed his hat on the rocker. "I didn't know if I'd arouse you or not," he said. "You put the candle up at the right moment."

He paced in front of the fireplace, opening and closing his hands the way he did when he felt pressed. Then suddenly he jammed his hands into his pockets and faced Daniel.

"Daniel," he said, "have you got any tea?"

"Tea!"

Beckett nodded. And then to make it worse, he added, "English tea."

How long had it been since anyone had felt free to drink tea or had dared to drink it openly? Even Tories abstained as a peaceful way of protesting the tax. In addition, it was healthier. There'd been a time when the Committee of Inspection searched a house if they expected tea was in it. Some tea had been smuggled in from Holland but it didn't taste the same and people were expected to do without.

But English tea!

"Well, do you or don't you?" Beckett snapped. "My mother said if anyone had tea, it would be Dr. West. He might have held some back, she said, so he could give it to folks who were sick. Is your father home?"

"No."

Beckett nodded as if he had hardly expected Dr. West to be in.

"In Boston, is he?"

"Yes." Everyone knew his father was neglecting his practice, running off every couple of weeks to visit his old friend, Mr. Blake, in Boston. Running away from his grief, folks said, running away from his memories and responsibilities, and it was time he settled down.

"Well, then, would you know?" Beckett insisted. "Is there any tea in the house?"

"I never knew my father to take tea on a sick call." Daniel sat down on a stool. "What is it, Beckett?" he asked. "Sit down and tell me. Who wants tea?"

"Judge Ropes." Beckett flung himself down on the hearth step. "He's real sick, Daniel. Real sick. Says the only thing he wants is a cup of English tea. Miranda called up to my mother."

Miranda was Judge Ropes' cook, a woman who had been with the family ever since the Judge and his wife had been married. Daniel could picture her in the white mobcap she always wore, hallooing from the middle of the street so as not to spread germs. It was harder to picture the Judge, such a stubborn, straight-walking, strong-speaking man, begging for a cup of tea.

Daniel stood up. "Let's go into the office," he said. Taking the lighted candle, he led the way to the front of the house. As soon as he set the candle down on his father's desk, however, he knew that this was not a likely place for tea. Everything was in the open here, within sight and handling of anyone who came into the room—all the herbs and ointments and medicines lined up and marked on the shelf or on the counter beside the bottle of leeches and the doctor's mortar and pestle. At the far end of the room was another

15

worktable with a pitcher and basin on it, and on a shelf underneath were the surgical instruments— birthing forceps, amputating tools, and the like. A pair of crutches leaned against the wall. The only other furniture was a desk and two chairs, and the desk held no secrets either—only medical books and papers.

"Nothing here," Daniel said. "And there'd be nothing in the cellar either. Only other place I can think of is the pie room."

Daniel had always called the spare room the pie room. People who had a spare room upstairs generally found it the coldest place for the winter's pie and pudding supply—the sixty or more mince pies and the dozens of plum puddings every housewife made during the two weeks before Thanksgiving.

Daniel and Beckett went upstairs, shutting the door quickly so the kitchen warmth wouldn't enter. Daniel set the candle down on a chest of drawers. He didn't like coming to this room. It had too much of his mother in it. She had finished the winter baking before she had had Jonathon, and Daniel had helped her spread planks across the bed where they had lined up rows of pies. He knew that Hannah served pies and puddings from this supply, but he had had no occasion to come into the room.

There were still some pies left on the bed, a few on the floor under the window, and there were four plum puddings on top of the sealskin trunk. Of course, he'd known they'd be here but he hadn't figured on the smell. The whole room smelled of the pies his mother had baked. Almost as fresh as the day she'd baked them.

Daniel clenched his fists. How *could* the pies still be there? he asked himself. Still smelling so mincey. And the puddings. How *dared* they? All of them placed as she had placed them. Surviving.

Quickly he went to a cupboard at the side of the room. He opened the doors, waiting a moment before he spoke.

"If there is any tea," he said at last, "this is a likely place."

One by one, Daniel and Beckett took the lids off the crocks. They smelled. Apple butter. Mincemeat. Sage. Fennel. There was no tea.

"Sorry," Daniel said. "I guess not."

Beckett sat down on the edge of the bed. He was working his hands again. "Daniel," he said. "Folks are mad at the Judge. Because he doesn't go to the Pest House. Daniel, he's too sick to go anywhere."

"Who's mad?"

"Liberty people. I heard the talk in town. They're just looking to fault him because he's a Tory. They claim he wants to get back at them for insisting he go against the new law and take his salary from the province instead of the crown. Daniel—"

"Yes?"

"They say he *wants* to spread the smallpox."

Daniel groaned. "After all the Judge has done for Salem, people can say that!"

"They can say anything. They can say the Judge has deliberately loosed his cat into the streets."

"The Judge never had a cat."

"I know."

"Oh, Beckett, let's think." Daniel cast about in his mind for friends who might have hidden some tea. Someone they could go to at this time of night.

"What about that trunk?" Beckett asked, pointing to the wall. "Any hope of some being hidden there?"

Daniel held out no hope but he moved the four plum puddings that were on the lid and he opened it. Just as he thought, the trunk was filled with folded materials—lengths of dress goods, summer quilts, extra sheets, shirting. Daniel thrust his hand down one side and struck something hard. He pushed aside the cloth and pulled out a large tin box. There was no marking on it. He pried off the lid and he smiled at Beckett. There was no mistaking the odor of tea. They held the tin up to their noses and breathed deeply.

"Ah-h," Beckett sighed. "I'd forgotten." He took another deep breath. "Do you suppose, Daniel . . . sometime . . . ?"

He didn't need to finish the sentence. Daniel grinned. "Maybe," he said. "Sometime."

While Beckett was sniffing, Daniel found an empty jar and filled it from the tin. "You know, Beckett," he said, "I'm glad of one thing. Folks can't visit a person with smallpox. No one can tell Judge Ropes what's being said about him. At least while he's sick, he won't know."

The two boys went out of the room but at the door to his bedroom Daniel stopped. "You wait for me in the kitchen," he said. "I'm going to put on my clothes and come along."

There wasn't apt to be *real* danger, Daniel told himself, shivering in the cold room as he got dressed. The Liberty Boys had done some pretty ornery things but so far nothing that would actually hurt a person. Still, he and Beckett would be no match for them and when they went out, it would be best not to meet anyone. Instead of walking in the middle of the street, the way a person normally would, they would stick to the shadows.

But as soon as Daniel and Beckett stepped out the back door, these plans were forgotten. The town was no longer quiet. The boys ran around the corner of the house to the main street, the part that was called Paved Street because it was the only street in town that was paved. To the right in the next block where Beckett and Judge Ropes lived lanterns were moving around. They didn't seem to be going anyplace—just back and forth, up and down. To the left there was nothing to see, only to hear. From the direction of the Common came the sound of singing. Daniel couldn't quite catch the words but he knew what they'd be. From the Liberty Song:

> "Our right arms are ready,
> Steady, men, steady!"

It was the Whigs celebrating the repeal of the stamp tax, acting as if it were *their* holiday, as if only *they* had a right to mark it.

Daniel and Beckett took to the middle of the road and ran to the right toward the lanterns. Ten or fifteen people were in front of Judge Ropes' house. They had coats on over nightclothes. Men had their bare feet thrust into boots; few had even taken time to put on hats. As Daniel and Beckett ran up, no one spoke. Mr. Foote, Beckett's father, simply pointed to Judge Ropes' house. It was dark except for a light in the kitchen on the right side. It took Daniel a minute to see what was wrong. Then he drew in his breath. Every window in the front of Judge Ropes' house was broken. Mr. Foote stepped closer and held up his lantern. Glass was strewn all over the lawn. Along with the glass were rocks and bricks; the rest, Daniel figured, were in the house.

Mr. Foote tried to describe what had happened but all that came out was how quick it had been. A gang evidently had crept up quietly, let loose all at once with the bricks and rocks they had come armed with, and by the time the neighbors were outside, they'd pounded off. It had all taken place, Daniel guessed, while he and Beckett were in the pie room.

"Didn't anyone go after them?" Daniel cried.

Mr. Foote nodded. "Yes. Nathaniel, the Judge's son. And some others. But they won't find them. By now they're all part of the big crowd celebrating on the Common."

Daniel looked around at the people standing on the street—neighbors, Whigs and Tories together, helpless, angry. Some of the women were crying; the men were pacing, talking in short shocked sentences.

Beckett stepped near the house. "Miranda!" he called. His voice didn't come out very loud but even so Daniel winced. It was as if the night itself had somehow been hurt and any sound, no matter what kind, was more than it could stand. Beckett waited a moment, then called louder. "Miranda! Come on out here. Daniel West has something for the Judge."

Slowly the kitchen door opened. At first there was just a square of light on the steps; then Miranda stepped out into the light, holding a lantern over her head and squinting nearsightedly at the street. Like everyone else, her clothes were in disarray and she wasn't wearing her mobcap. Her shoulders sagging, she obviously didn't know or care that under the lantern folks could see that she was all but bald.

"They've gone, Miranda," Beckett said gently. "It's all right. We're all friends here." Daniel set the jar down in the middle of the street, then everyone backed up while Miranda walked slowly out from the house. It was the only way a person could send something into a smallpox house without spreading the disease. The line of onlookers, backed up as far as they could, stood quietly and respectfully as Miranda approached the jar.

As she bent down, Mrs. Foote spoke. "Tell the Judge, Miranda, that the damage was done by a few ruffians. Tell him the town loves him."

Miranda straightened up. "I did tell him that, Mrs. Foote."

"What did he say?"

"He didn't say anything. His heart is broken."

Miranda made her way back to the house. No one moved until the kitchen door closed.

Then Captain Pickering spoke. He was one of the town's leading Whigs and a good friend of the Judge.

"What was in that jar?" he asked.

Daniel was standing on the edge of the group. He whirled around.

"Tea!" he shouted. "It was a blasted jar of English tea!"

He shoved his hands into the pockets of his greatcoat and turned toward town. He wasn't going home. He was going to find Jeremy Packer.

Chapter Two

DANIEL DIDN'T bother to stick to streets. He cut through back lots and across gardens in the direction of the waterfront, where Jeremy was likely to be at this time of night. He didn't even try to avoid the burying ground. He walked right past as if it were daytime instead of night. He was approaching Derby Wharf when he heard Jeremy's cry.

"Twelve o'clock!" Jeremy called. He waited a

moment, then he raised his great rolling sailor's voice, letting it out as if it were a rope and he was seeing how far he could cast it. "And all's well!"

"All's well, is it?" Daniel muttered. It was the first time that Jeremy Packer had ever made him mad. It was the first time that Jeremy's being a Whig had made any difference to him.

Daniel broke into a run. Sometimes Jeremy was carried away by the sound of his voice and he repeated himself. As Daniel reached the wharf, he saw Jeremy, his lantern in his hand, his back to the sea. He was halfway down the wharf, facing Salem, just standing and facing it, the way a preacher faces his congregation. As Daniel's feet hit the wooden plankings of the dock, Jeremy began again. "Twelve o'clock!"

"No!" Daniel called. "Don't say it!" His own voice was small and breathless, lost in the rattle of the plankings, but he reached Jeremy in time.

Jeremy lowered his lantern and stepped forward. "What's wrong, lad?"

Daniel had lost so much breath that all he could do was to stand, panting, while in the distance, toward the Common, snatches of liberty song and liberty laughter rang in the air.

"What's wrong?" Jeremy repeated.

Daniel shook his arm toward the Common. "*That's* wrong!" he exploded. "*That's* wrong! You're shouting 'All's well' and up there your friends—your *friends*— are putting Salem to shame again. Like in the witch days." He dropped his arm. "How can you be a Whig, Jeremy? How can you?"

24

Daniel blurted out the whole story of Judge Ropes and by the time he'd finished, his anger at Jeremy was gone. Daniel knew well enough that the Liberty Boys were only a small, wild group among the Whigs, young men who would in any case be looking for mischief and only used the Tories as an excuse. Jeremy and Captain Pickering and Mr. Derby—the true Sons of Liberty—all of them were embarrassed by the Liberty Boys.

But Jeremy wasn't thinking of the Liberty Boys; he was thinking of Judge Ropes. "Poor man," he murmured. "Poor man. Tomorrow we'll have to send him a letter. The self-respecting Whigs, that is. Saying we're sorry. Saying we appreciate him. That poor man. And his wife, too. And a one-year-old child in the house." He put his arm around Daniel. "All is not well, after all, is it, lad?" He turned Daniel to face the sea and the two walked slowly toward the end of the dock.

Daniel knew that looking out to sea gave Jeremy comfort. He'd been a sailor for thirty years and he always said that looking at the sea rested his eyes from the sight of people getting in each other's way. Jeremy sat down on a barrel at the end of the dock and motioned to Daniel to seat himself on another. He reached into his pocket and took out a poke of raisin cookies and the little flask he carried filled with apple cider. Daniel thought that one of Tillie's cookies was more comfort than the sea, but even as he munched, he tried to find the peace that Jeremy found in the sea. He couldn't. The sea just stretched away, gray, toward

25

nothing and answered none of his questions. And Daniel had questions.

"Jeremy," he said at last, "why can't we just pay for the tea and stop all this bickering?"

Jeremy didn't move. "If a man drew a sword on you," he said slowly, "and if you broke that sword, would you feel called upon to pay for it?"

For a moment Daniel felt another flash of anger. "Maybe," he wanted to say. "Maybe, if it would stop the bickering." After all, it was the people Daniel's age that were going to be pulled into that bickering. And the bickering could go on and on and on unless someone stopped it. It could go on and on, using up all of Daniel's youth, spoiling the best years of his whole life. He shivered.

Jeremy turned to him sharply. "You're cold, boy. Let's get you home." He stood up but before leaving, he uncorked his flask, stepped to the edge of the wharf, and held the flask high.

"To the King!" he said. It was one thing they could agree on. He took a drink, then handed the flask to Daniel, who was standing now too. For a moment Daniel listened to the water lapping against the pilings, and he felt ashamed of himself. Not only for his anger but for his thoughts. Draping the future in black, that's what he'd been doing.

"To the King!" Daniel repeated.

After all, everyone, Whigs and Tories alike, were loyal to the king. It was only on the authority of Parliament they differed. Deep down, they were all Englishmen as well as Americans. Suddenly it seemed a grand

26

thing to be standing on the end of Derby Wharf at midnight drinking a toast to the king on the other side of all that water, at the far end of the triangle. He pictured the king, sitting on his throne, thinking kindly thoughts about his colonies, already regretting the mistakes Lord North had made. Daniel's heart swelled with pride. The line between Salem and London seemed so short that he halfway wondered if the king couldn't sense there were two people drinking his health on Derby Wharf—one of them a bony fourteen-year-old boy of middling height, shivering in his great-coat, the other a burly man bundled up for his night duties with a scarf tied around his head and a three-cornered hat pulled down on top of that. Only the three corners had mostly disappeared and the hat was shaped more like a squashed pie riding above a pair of bushy gray eyebrows. Daniel put the flask to his mouth and drank.

"Jeremy," he said as they started back down the wharf, "I don't want to go home. Let me go on your rounds with you."

"You're half frozen now, boy. And what would your father say? Does he know you're out?"

They were walking past the shed warehouses built on either side of the wharf and Jeremy was peering in the windows, checking for fire. It was the chief duty of the night watchman, looking for fire and raising the alarm if he found one.

"My father's not home."

"In Boston again, eh?" Daniel knew Jeremy was try-ing to make his voice sound easy, as if it were only

27

natural for a boy's father to take off for Boston every few days without any real explanation.

"He's very friendly with Mr. Blake," Daniel said stiffly.

Jeremy grunted.

"Maybe he and Mr. Blake are working on something," Daniel suggested.

"Maybe."

"Maybe they're working in politics. Maybe with the governor." Daniel had never thought of such a thing before but as he heard himself say it, he felt better.

Jeremy only grunted.

"Well, you Whigs are always meeting secretly. I guess the other side can too."

"Did you leave Sarah asleep?"

"She's staying with the Widow Ray."

Jeremy shook his head. "She's persistent, that widow. Getting in with you folks any way she can, isn't she?"

"Yep." Daniel didn't like to think of the Widow Ray or any of the other widows in town, the way they hung around his father, saying what he needed was a new wife. "It's not only Sarah she's gone after," he said. "She's sicked Peter on to me."

Peter Ray, the widow's son, was in Daniel's class in school, an obnoxious specimen if there ever was one, and every time Daniel turned around recently, it seemed, Peter was there, toadying up to him.

Jeremy chuckled. "Maybe that's why your father goes to Boston. To get away from the widow. I wouldn't blame him."

They were on land now, walking slowly, circling

outbuildings where fires were most likely to start. Every so often Jeremy stopped and sniffed the air. He was always worrying because he couldn't be every place at once and complaining that Salem needed more than one night watchman.

"Jeremy?"

"Yes, boy?"

"You going to let me go with you tonight? I've always wanted to—"

"What, boy?"

"I've always wanted to see Salem through a whole night. I've always wanted to be with you at the North Bridge when dawn comes. You know, when you sing out the hour and say the sun's up and tell the weather." He hesitated. "Maybe there on the North Bridge we could drink another toast to the king."

When Jeremy didn't answer, Daniel went on. "I'm warmer now that we're walking. There's no reason—"

"You've got school tomorrow, lad."

"I'll be all right."

They were going up toward the Common. The crowd had evidently dispersed. Some stragglers were still on the streets, others were stopping off at taverns, and a few greeted Jeremy as they passed. A group of rather furtive-looking characters in fishermen's hats swung around the corner and disappeared into the night.

"You recognize them?" Daniel asked.

"Look like Marbleheaders."

"Marbleheaders." Daniel rolled the word as if it tasted bad in his mouth. "Yea. Marbleheaders. What are they doing here at this time of night?" But before Daniel had the question out of his mouth, he had jumped at the answer. He looked at Jeremy and knew he was thinking the same thing. Marblehead, the town next door, just across the bay, was not like Salem. It was a rough place and Marbleheaders were always causing trouble, trying to prove they were better than Salem folks. They were even claiming that Salem had tried to spread the smallpox to them. "Maybe," Daniel began. "Maybe . . ."

He didn't need to say any more. Jeremy nodded.

"I bet it would make the Judge feel better," Daniel said, "if he knew that a bunch of Marbleheaders were in town tonight." He put his hand on Jeremy's arm. "Jeremy, let's go over there. Let's rouse Miranda. Let's not let the Judge go on thinking that it was his own town that turned against him."

Jeremy shook his head. "We don't know that for sure, boy. And tomorrow's time enough. On my rounds, I may pick up more information. Proof, even."

Daniel tried not to notice that Jeremy had used the first person, singular. "*I* may be able to pick up information," he had said; not *we*. Maybe it was a slip of the tongue. Surely Jeremy meant to take him because instead of turning left on King Street, as they would to go to Daniel's house, Jeremy was going right toward the Common.

Daniel often thought the Common occupied the same place in the town as a kitchen occupied in a house. It was the place where the real living was done. Maybe history was written down in the Town House, but more often than not it was acted out on the Common. The Salem Common was not like the common in some small towns, a little bandana of cropped green with only a tree or two, a few benches, and a flagpole, big enough for a muster only if the men in the last row kept their back ends sucked in. When the militia was reviewed in Salem, only a part of the Common was used; the rest of it went off wild with a whole string of little ponds for boys to fish in, with trysting places for lovers, with berry spots and mushroom patches and bogs blue with iris in the spring and thick with cattails in the fall. There were hills for sled riding, hidey-holes for boys to try out their first tobacco and walks where sailors could get the feel of the land again. Grown folks complained about the sloppiness of the Common, the mud and the weeds and the tangle of brush, but you wouldn't hear a boy complain. What could be better than a piece of sloppy nature right in the middle of a neat, fenced-up town?

But it wasn't all fun on the Common. He'd seen the flags flying at half-mast too many times—for captains lost at sea, leaders dead, for bad news from England. Then there was that awful day several years back when a man they called an Informer had been tarred and feathered on the militia grounds. He'd been like an animal, stripped of everything human, his eyes gone white and wild, his body thick with black tar, and no matter which way he'd run, people had thrown feathers at him. One group had even thrown a live goose.

They were at the Common now. Jeremy was right,

Daniel thought, to come here. Perhaps there'd still be someone with news of the Marbleheaders. But there was no one under the chestnut tree where people generally gathered for meetings. At least, there was no real person. If Daniel had thought about it, he would have known the celebrants would have left something behind, but Daniel was thinking only of Judge Ropes as he glanced up at the tree. Dangling from one of the branches was a pair of legs. There was no mistaking it; there were boots on the ends of the legs. Jeremy saw it too and raised his lantern. It was an entire body hanging by the neck from a rope but by Jeremy's lantern it was immediately apparent it was not a real body. A man's clothes had been stuffed with straw and a scarecrow head added. A sign pinned to the body read: LET THE NORTH WIND BLOW. Then under it: STAMP TAX YESTERDAY, TEA TAX TOMORROW. It was an effigy of Lord North.

Jeremy grinned. "Just what he deserves." He lowered his lantern and started across the field, looking, he said, for any traces of bonfires that might have been lit during the night. Daniel followed, trying to rid his mind of the picture of that swinging body. He didn't mind seeing such a thing in the daytime but it was like the burying ground; the night changed it. Daniel kept his eyes on the ground, avoiding the sight of trees altogether until on the way back toward the edge of the woods he saw Jeremy stop, look up, and then let loose with a low whistle.

Daniel steadied himself. "Not another effigy?"

"No. Not this time."

Daniel looked up. It wasn't a stuffed body; it was a real body. It was a dead cat hanging from a rope. Tied around its neck was a note. THIS CAT HANGS BY A ROPE, IN PLACE OF A ROPES. A POX ON ALL TORIES!

"Marbleheaders," Daniel whispered.

"Maybe."

"It has to be." Daniel tried to control his shivering so Jeremy wouldn't see. "No man in Salem would do that."

Jeremy sighed and handed his lantern to Daniel. "There are mean men in Salem too, you know, boy." He reached into his pocket for a knife to cut down the cat. "And I don't know why you say 'no *man*' in Salem." Jeremy cut the rope and the body of the cat fell with a thud on the hard ground. "It could be boys. Some of these so-called Liberty Boys may be no older than you are."

It was a new idea to Daniel. He'd always pictured the Liberty Boys as big, strapping nineteen- and twenty-year-olds, some of them even older with records of thievery and the like.

"Would you know any of them?" Daniel asked.

"I have my suspicions." Jeremy was on his hands and knees, taking the note off the cat and pushing the body under some brush and leaves. He was breathing heavily. "But about this cat," he said. "Hearing about this won't help the Judge. Neither he nor anyone else will hear about it from me."

"Nor from me," Daniel whispered.

Jeremy stood up. "Well, I'm going to take you to my house now, boy. And you're going to sleep the rest of

the night in a warm kitchen with your brother Jonathon."

Daniel started to protest but he could see it was no
use.

"I'll leave a note for Hannah as I go by later,"
Jeremy said, "so she won't worry." He squeezed
Daniel's arm. "I'll take you with me on my rounds
another time, when it gets warmer."

Now that there was no use in pretending to be
warm, Daniel gave himself up to the weather. He put
his gloved hands over his ears, then over his nose, and
finally he put both hands together in the same glove in
the hope that one would draw heat from the other.
Jeremy quickened his steps, cutting through the Common, up Ferry Lane, and west to St. Peter's Church,
the church that Daniel went to, on the corner of
Prison Street.

"No danger of fire here," Daniel said. "Nothing
going on at the church tonight."

"No?" Jeremy raised his lantern. Long fingers of
light played up and down the big oak doors, then
settled in a pool on the top step. There in front of the
church, almost against the door, was a pile of slops.
The lantern held firm. Potato peelings, eggshells,
rotten apple cores, chicken feathers, and what smelled
like spoiled fish.

"On the church steps!" Daniel whispered. "The
church steps!"

Jeremy sighed. "It's the Tory church, lad. The
Church of England. You know that."

"Tory church!" Daniel jumped up the step and began kicking the slop into the street. "Tory churches! Whig churches!" His breath hung on the cold air in little frosted explosions. "Is everything to be divided?" He stepped down and kicked his boot against the young butternut tree growing by the corner of the church. "This is a Tory tree, I suppose." He pointed down at his boot. "And this boot. Is it a Tory boot because I'm wearing it?" Suddenly he felt as if he were being pushed into a room and everything he'd ever touched was being thrown in after him. He wasn't Daniel West any more, a boy who happened to be a Tory. He was a Tory who happened to be Daniel West.

"Easy, boy, easy." Jeremy took him by the elbow and steered him to the street.

Daniel stopped to stamp off the mess that still stuck to his boots. When some of it wouldn't shake off, he picked up a twig from the ground and scraped at his boot. "One thing," he muttered. "This slop on my boot. That's Whig slop. Pure Whig slop."

Jeremy laughed. "Looks like it to me, lad. It looks Whig all right."

The two walked on without speaking, stepping wide of the holes and ruts in the road, swinging to the left and right of slippery patches. They were almost to Jeremy's house when Jeremy stopped and faced Daniel. His lantern made a circle of light on the ground and in the center of that circle Jeremy's and Daniel's boots stood toe to toe.

Jeremy cleared his throat. "Daniel, I just want you to know something. Between you and me there'll never be any Whig or Tory. Understand? And when you step in that door"—he pointed to his kitchen—"it's not a Whig or Tory house you'll be entering. It's home. An extra home. Everyone needs a spare home or two."

Daniel's boots moved over beside Jeremy's as they both turned toward the kitchen door. "I know, Jeremy," he said quietly. "I know. I wasn't sounding off against you. I was carried away. Judge Ropes and all." He kicked a clump of ice in his path. "The trouble's never seemed so serious. There've been threats and mischief before and talk. But tonight—" Daniel shivered. "Tonight it's as if there were blood in the air."

Jeremy nodded. "The news is so long coming from England," he said. "Tempers are short. And you're tired, lad. And cold." He opened the door.

As soon as Daniel stepped into Jeremy's kitchen, the world fell into its familiar shape and was at peace again. The fire in the hearth had settled down for the night; it was at that comfortable stage with none of the frantic flames of a fresh fire or the sputterings of a dying one. The whole room had taken on a faintly rosy glow and even the furniture had an air of resting. It was strange, Daniel thought, how a room you loved had a foreverness about it, as if the fixings had grown there—Tillie's spinning wheel in one corner, the blue rag rug on the floor, the pine table before the window, the rocker, the yellow curtains, the iron trivets on the wall. Everything was somehow just as it was *meant* to be. Even Jonathon's cradle before the fire. And Jonathon.

Daniel walked straight to the cradle. He smiled. If it was a healing thing to come into Jeremy's kitchen, it was downright warming to gaze at a baby brother. Jonathon was lying on his side, one hand curled loosely on top of the covers. Daniel took off his gloves and started to slip a finger into the little hole that Jonathon's hand made, but then he realized his finger would be cold and he drew it back.

Jeremy was beside Daniel. "He's going to look like you, lad."

"Me?" Daniel grinned and pushed his hat to the back of his head as he considered Jonathon further. In the midst of his considerations the bedroom door opened. Tillie put her head around the corner.

"Thought I heard voices," she said. "I'll be right out."

She closed the door and when she came out again she was dressed in a long cotton gown. Her gray hair hung in two braids over her shoulder, giving her almost a girlish appearance which was difficult to get used to. Tillie was not normally girlish-looking. She was a big, angular woman with a long bony face, high cheekbones, a deep voice, and hair drawn severely to the back of her head. It was not until you looked in her eyes that you saw that deep inside this big plain woman there was someone small and soft and gentle, someone who longed for children of her own to fuss over. Not

37

that she'd admit it. Feelings, she seemed to think, were not becoming to a woman her size.

"Well, Jeremy," she said, striding to the fire to poke it up, "where'd you pick up this stray?" She jerked her thumb in Daniel's direction.

"On Derby Wharf." Jeremy grinned. "Thought we could bed him down beside his brother."

Tillie held out her hands for Daniel's coat and hat. "Reckon we can." She went into the bedroom and came back with two comforts.

Daniel pulled off his boots and rolled up in the comforts. He listened to Jeremy go out and to Tillie's bedroom door closing; then he reached out his hand and very gently began rocking the cradle. It was the first time he'd been alone in a room with his brother. As he rocked, he found himself talking, telling Jonathon how it would be when he came home. It was one of the things his father didn't speak of but Daniel had his own ideas about it. Now in the flickering firelight he confided to Jonathon what he hoped would take place. He described how his father could build an addition to their house, how Jeremy and Tillie could move in and be there to take care of Jonathon not only now but always. The way he told it, it seemed to him he could see Jonathon and Jeremy and Tillie already there. He could see Jonathon older, going fishing with him and his father. He could see Tillie frying their catch, laughing and joking the way his mother used to.

When he finally fell asleep, it was into one of those deep sleeps when a few hours seems like a long night. He was awakened by Jonathon's cry and then by Tillie calling to him to pick up the baby while she got dressed.

The morning light was graying at the windows. Daniel wrapped a blanket around Jonathon and was settling into the rocker when Jeremy's voice floated into the room.

"Six o'clock!" he called.

Daniel waited for Jeremy to go on and tell the world the sun was up and what kind of weather was in the making. But Jeremy didn't go on. He didn't say anything more.

Tillie came in and walked to the window. "The weather doesn't look that bad," she said, "that he can't talk about it."

She went to the table and it seemed to Daniel she made an abnormal racket, clanking the lid on the teakettle, beating at a bowl of batter.

"Something's wrong," Daniel said. "Else he'd go on."

"I know." Tillie slapped the teakettle over the fire. "We'll know soon. Only takes a few minutes to get here from the North Bridge."

Indeed, something was wrong. As soon as Jeremy stepped in the door, Daniel and Tillie both knew it. Daniel was standing now, still holding Jonathon.

"What is it?" he said.

But Tillie put her arm out between Daniel and Jeremy. "If it's bad news," she said, "I want Daniel to put Jonathon down before you tell it. It's unlucky to hear bad news while you're holding a baby."

Jeremy nodded. "Put the baby down, boy."

Daniel lowered Jonathon into the cradle and it was

not until he had straightened up that Jeremy spoke. He stood still in the middle of the room and spoke through lips stiff with cold.

"Judge Ropes died," he said. "A couple of hours ago."

Daniel swallowed. "Did you—" he began.

Jeremy shook his head. "I didn't find out anything. I didn't tell him anything. The Judge died in his bed with the wind whistling in the broken windows at either side of him."

Chapter Three

S ALEM WAS a sober place the day of Judge Ropes'
death. Soon after Jeremy announced the hour from
the North Bridge, the bells of St. Peter's Church began
to toll, the slow ponderous ring that proclaimed the
death of an important citizen—nine times to indi-
cate that it was a man who had died, then slowly forty-
eight times to tell his age. It was like a march, those

bells—each ring a heavy footstep starting from the belfry, resounding through the skies, returning never.

The bells set the tone for the day. Lord North's effigy still dangled from the chestnut tree in the Common but it was not the target for stones it would have been, had the temper of the town been different. People didn't pay Lord North much attention; where they stopped was at the flagpole. Sometime during the day everyone, it seemed, went past the flagpole. Everyone but Judge Ropes. That was the saddest thing of all, Daniel thought. There was the flag halted halfway up its mast in sorrow over the Judge and he couldn't see it, nor could he see all the men, Tory and Whig both, who took off their hats as they went by.

Later the town behaved the way a person does when he feels guilty. At first there was shock and quiet and kindness and tears. That was Stage One. Then after a week or so it was as if the whole town, in a single body, hitched up its belt and swore not to do wrong again. Like an erring boy who thinks everything will be all right if only he makes resolutions enough. This was Stage Two. Men gathered in taverns and talked of forming a committee to patrol the streets at night. Peter Frye, a Tory judge accused of not crossing the Liberty Boys for fear of personal reprisal, stood up in Town Meeting, jangled the ring of keys on the end of his watch chain, and declaimed on civic responsibility. All over Salem, fathers admonished sons to be gentlemen, and schoolteachers, anxious to do their part, applied the rod more freely.

To show how far people were willing to go in this

stage, they even listened to old Mr. "Ding-Dong" Allison's curfew talk. Daniel could scarcely believe his eyes the afternoon he and Jeremy went past the Common and saw Ding-Dong standing on a stump and at least fifteen people gathered around him, not jeering, not laughing, but *listening,* actually nodding their heads, some of them, as if they thought old Ding-Dong could make sense, as if they hadn't known him all their lives, as if they hadn't in their younger days fought him in his own war.

As long as anyone could remember, old Mr. Allison had been waging a war. His enemy was the younger generation. A stranger hearing him sound off on curfews might think he was a dirty, wild-eyed, whiskered, half-breed, tattered old man who was, nonetheless, excessively fond of law and order. Salem people knew better; at least up until now they had known that Mr. Ding-Dong Allison simply needed to hate. He'd picked on the young people and, of course, the young people couldn't be blamed for fighting back. Daniel and Beckett were part not of one generation but of two generations of boys who had made it a point of honor not to go past Mr. Allison's shack near the North River without making a few bell-like noises or otherwise recognizing his existence in an appropriate way.

And now here were men like Mr. Palfrey, the sailmaker, and Jonathon Murray, the cooper, weighing old Ding-Dong's words as if they . . . as if they had weight!

Daniel stopped at the back of the group and put his

hand on Jeremy's arm. "You suppose he's got a new text?" he asked.

Jeremy shook his head. "Same man," he said shortly. "Same talk. Only right now the town is ripe for it."

Ding-Dong had his hands on his knees and he was leaning toward the group as if he were telling them a secret.

"The young folks in this town," he said, "they're going to get us all in trouble. Deep trouble. You think this Judge Ropes thing is bad?" He fixed his attention on the members of the audience until he had them all nodding. "Well now," Ding-Dong said triumphantly, "that ain't nothin'. Nothin'. The young folks in this town are just warming up, let me tell you."

Normally by this time a crowd of boys would have gathered and have ding-donged old Mr. Allison right off his perch. The few boys who had stopped today, however, seemed to have sensed the atmosphere and had already slunk off. Only Edward Pine and Sam White stood on the sidelines. They were two fifteen-year-old apprentices who worked down at the waterfront. They were slouched against a tree trunk, picking their teeth, and exchanging sly looks.

"Now I tell you, friends," Mr. Allison went on, "young folks are bad enough in normal times but now they've got provocation. Unless we can get rid of the Tory element in town, no telling what young folks may do."

Daniel and Jeremy exchanged glances. Ding-Dong had rung in a change in his text, after all. He had added the Tories to his list of hates.

"In order to make this town safe," Ding-Dong went on, "we've got to make it one hundred percent Whig. We don't want young Tories running about, stirring up the patriotic folks. Roaming the streets after dark."

Suddenly he raised up on his toes and pointed a finger. "And that means you, Daniel West. I seen you out the night Judge Ropes died."

Everyone turned and stared at Daniel. Edward Pine and Sam White spit out their toothpicks and grinned.

Daniel was rooted to the ground. So many impulses flared up in him at exactly the same instant, he was unable to single one out and act on it. On the one hand, he wanted to go over to Sam White and Edward Pine and punch them both in the nose. On the other hand, he wanted to punch Mr. Allison in the nose. He felt Jeremy's hand firm on his elbow but before he could say anything, Mr. Allison went on.

"We all know Daniel's a Tory all right, but maybe we didn't know what a high-stepping Tory he is. He's a real tax-loving Tory." He raised his voice and the next words he laid down slowly, one by one. "Otherwise," he said, "he wouldn't have had tea in his house, now would he?"

"Shame!" It was Jeremy's voice that thundered out "Shame!" And now again, "Shame!" he cried—at old Mr. Allison, at the listeners, at Edward Pine and Sam White, who had already let loose a guffaw. "Tea for a dying man!" Jeremy cried. "From a doctor's house! Shame!"

The crowd shuffled off, looking rather abashed for listening to Mr. Allison. Jeremy steered Daniel away from the Common, walking him so fast, he didn't have a chance to think if he wanted to stay and carry out any of his impulses or not.

"You did fine, lad," Jeremy said as he finally slowed up near the waterfront. "Best thing is not to answer back. You can't go wrong acting like a gentleman."

"Gentleman!" Daniel pulled his arm free of Jeremy. "I wasn't being a gentleman. I was just being slow." He jammed his hands into the pockets of his greatcoat. "I should have spoken my own piece and not left it to you. I should have knocked Sam White's and Edward Pine's heads together. I should have ding-donged Mr. Allison all the way into the North River." Daniel stopped for breath and then went on more slowly. "I should have said I was proud to be a Tory. And glad to have had that tea."

They were at the water now. Mr. Derby's brigantine, *Neptune*, had come in that morning from the West Indies and the dock was abustle with activity—men unloading, rolling out barrels of molasses, tossing bundles to one another, greeting townsmen, shouting, joking. Normally, Daniel would have been caught up in the excitement. Any ship that came fresh into the harbor carried, as part of its cargo, the breath of life itself—the taste, feel, smell of life far away which in turn seemed to quicken the pulse of life on shore. It lasted only a few hours, this quickening, a day at most. As the real cargo was unloaded and became part and parcel of the town itself, so this indefinable current of excitement was absorbed by the great blanket of air that people breathed regularly.

46

Daniel saw the excitement flickering in Jeremy's eyes. "Go on down to the dock, Jeremy," he said. "You know most of the men. Go on down and talk to them. Take a close look at the *Neptune* before the foreignness wears off."

Some of the seamen had spotted Jeremy and were already hailing him.

"Go on," Daniel urged. "I'll wait here. Go on."

Jeremy didn't make a move. He put one foot up on a keg marked SALT and said maybe he'd go and maybe he wouldn't. "What if that Sam White and that Edward Pine come down this way?" he asked. "What are you going to do? You going to get into an altercation with them?"

Daniel sighed and, leaning against a molasses barrel, looked out to sea, past Cat Cove and Winter Island. He squinted his eyes as if he might be seeing beyond the Misery Islands, even across the miles to London itself. "No, I guess not," he said at last. "Likely I've caused my father enough trouble. Breaking out that tea." He turned to Jeremy. "You can see, everyone knows about it."

"So?"

"Remember how Judge Frye's name was read out in disgrace at every Town Meeting for months when he was found with tea?"

"He wasn't a doctor."

"No," Daniel agreed. "But he was a Tory. That's all that matters, I'm thinking. I'm a Tory."

Jeremy took his foot off the keg of salt. "What you are, lad," he said gently, "is a worrier. You're borrow-

47

ing trouble. Time enough when it comes." He put his hand on Daniel's shoulder. "I'll go down the dock for a few minutes," he said. "You wait here."

Watching Jeremy go off with such a springy step, Daniel tried to feel the excitement. He took long, deep breaths but all he smelled was Salem at low tide. He turned his attention back to shore. At one side of him some eight- and nine-year-old boys were squatted down before barrels. They had paper straws stuck in bung holes and their cheeks were caved in with the effort of sucking and pulling the heavy molasses through the straws. Every once in a while one would stop and grin and run his tongue around his mouth.

On the other side of the dock more children were stooped, looking into an enormous crate. Daniel walked over. Inside the crate was one of those giant green turtles that were used to make soup so fashionable now to serve at parties. This one had a tag on it. COLONEL WILLIAM BROWNE, it said. At least, Daniel thought, this turtle would end up in Tory soup. Colonel Browne was the leading citizen of Salem, the most lavish entertainer, and a Tory. Daniel watched the children poke sticks through the slats, tapping on the turtle's thick armor, trying to reach under to tickle the turtle's belly. All at once from one end of the armor the turtle extended its neck, a wrinkled cord with two tiny eyes imbedded in it. The children screamed with laughter and poked their sticks until the neck disappeared again. Daniel shivered. The eyes in that monstrous-looking, armor-backed turtle were not too different from any eyes. They reminded him of the eyes of Peter Ray, the widow's son. They had that same dumb, pleading look.

When Daniel looked up from the crate, Jeremy was beside him.

"You didn't stay long," Daniel observed.

"Saw everything I wanted to."

"Hear anything?"

Jeremy nodded. "The *Neptune* bespoke a brig from London, New York-bound, the other day."

"Well?"

"Everyone in London is talking about our Tea Party. Some good talk. Some bad."

"What did the king say?"

"Hadn't said anything when the brig left six weeks ago. But Parliament was expected to make an announcement momentarily."

"That means we could hear any day."

"Yep."

After all this time, Daniel thought. The Tea Party had been December 16th and you had to count on six to eight weeks for a ship to take the news to London. Then you had to allow the king and Parliament some weeks to discuss the news and decide what to do. Then there was another six to eight weeks to bring their decision back. No matter what the weather was, it appeared that spring was about here.

"And if the news isn't to the liking of you Whigs—" Daniel began. He was staring down at the crate and the children bent before it. And suddenly, for no reason at all, Daniel picked up one of the boys by the collar. "You quit tormenting that turtle," he said. "You hear?"

As soon as Daniel put the boy down, he was ashamed. What was the matter with him anyway? Acting like an old man. It wasn't as if he cared what happened to a green turtle with eyes like Peter Ray's.

"Let's go home, Jeremy," he said.

Afterward when he looked back on it, Daniel realized that Stage Three, the final stage after Judge Ropes' death, began the day the *Neptune* arrived with its rumor from London. It was only a little rumor, of course, but people had been so news-starved all winter that they took that rumor and worked over it in taverns, in kitchens, on street corners, until after a while the Whigs had turned it one way and the Tories had turned it another. Nobody noticed that while they were pulling and stretching at this one little rumor, the patrol talk and the curfew talk and the gentleman talk had dwindled and the grieving over Judge Ropes had stopped altogether. The smallpox talk stopped too; Judge Ropes was the last case of the winter's epidemic. Stage Three was Back to Normal, Whig versus Tory.

The change became most apparent, perhaps, on the first real spring day. Right out of the middle of winter and mud and wind it bloomed, one of those perfect days that seem to have been created on another planet not plagued by the evil that lies beside the good on this planet or by the sorrow that is a tail to joy. They say it is just such a day that melancholy people find unbearable; the outer world shows such promise and man, himself—what is he? Against all that glory, man seems a pretty piddling creature with a talent only for messing things up. In any case, the frustrations in Salem were magnified by the day, by the sight of scraggly willow trees suddenly dripping a fresh yellow-green, by the sight of budding maples blushing pink in the sunlight, by the sight of jack-in-the-pulpits popping up in the Common.

Daniel looked out the kitchen window and saw an early robin rocking on a branch of the hawthorn tree. A person could take such pleasure in the day, he thought, if only it weren't for the Whigs! He turned to the table where his father and his sister, Sarah, were being served breakfast by Hannah.

"*Why* does there have to be such a commotion about a silly little tea tax?" he asked. He addressed the room at large, not really expecting an answer from anybody.

Hannah was at the fireplace, turning over the breakfast hotcakes. She was a hearty, matronly woman who had long ago given up the idea of having a husband in this town where women so outnumbered the men. Instead she cooked for others and saved her earnings for her old age—a lovely time, she said, when she would do nothing but gather shells to ornament the baskets she liked to make.

Dr. West sat at the kitchen table, looking down at his plate, cutting up his hotcakes into neat, tiny squares. He had a way recently of concentrating excessively on small, insignificant acts as if this would keep him from thinking about the bigger aspects of

51

his life, maybe even from thinking about Daniel himself. Had Dr. West been a small man, this meticulous behavior might have seemed appropriate, but he was broad and tall and it made Daniel uncomfortable to see him so picayune.

"It isn't a silly tea tax." It was Daniel's sister, Sarah, who tossed back her curls and answered him. She pursed her lips. "Shouldn't a mother expect anything of her children? The Widow Ray says England is just like our mother."

"Indeed? Well, when I want to hear what the Widow Ray thinks," Daniel snapped, "I'll ask her." Sarah had got so she set his teeth on edge. Eight years old and she had developed all the ways of a middle-aged busybody. Of the Widow Ray, to be exact. Sarah had always taken on the manner of the people she associated with, Daniel thought. "You shouldn't be running over to the Widow Ray's all the time," he said. "You'll be getting to look like her and we wouldn't want that."

Hannah chuckled. "She already smells like her," she said, referring to the anise drops that Sarah was always sucking when she came back from the widow's.

Sarah tossed her curls again but before she could say anything, Dr. West put down his knife and fork, crossing them methodically over his plate of squared-up hotcakes. "You were asking about the tea tax, Daniel," he said. He took off his spectacles, cleaned them, then leaned back in his chair, indicating that he was getting ready to answer Daniel's question at length, a question that Daniel had passed out as a simple remark, certainly not because he wanted a lecture. But here was his father going through all that old business about England needing money to pay for the French and Indian War she'd fought for our benefit and we had no call to be talking about representation when there were so many places in England that weren't represented in Parliament. It would be nice to have the tax lifted, of course. Indeed, he said, he hoped it would be and another way would be found to help England with her debts. But if it wasn't, all a person could do was to go along with the tax, and this was no real hardship.

Daniel looked at his father curiously. Did he really think after all this time that Daniel didn't know this? And believe it? To occupy his mind while his father was discoursing, Daniel looked out the window at the hawthorn tree. Each year the members of the family guessed what date the buds on the hawthorn tree would come into flower. No one had mentioned it this year. It was as if they were all afraid to pick up life the way it had once been.

"This country isn't ready to govern itself," Dr. West was saying but there was no fire in his voice; he was talking like a schoolmaster, walking over old ground, using other people's words.

Daniel leaned forward. "I'll give the hawthorn tree three weeks," he said. "How about you? Any bets this year?"

Dr. West started to glance at the window, then abruptly he shifted his eyes back to his plate and remarked that Samuel Adams, the leader of the Whigs in Boston, couldn't even keep himself out of debt.

"I don't care about Samuel Adams," Daniel snapped but his father paid no attention. He was talking in his schoolmaster's voice about Boston being the center of trouble as though Daniel were a child or as though he'd been in the Hebrides all winter while his father had been making his mysterious trips.

At the thought of Boston, however, Daniel began to pay stricter attention to the conversation. The night before, his father had returned from another of his trips and, as usual, he had volunteered no information about it.

Daniel watched for an opportunity to speak. He was glad that when it came, they were alone. Sarah had left the table and Hannah was getting her ready for Dame School.

"Did you enjoy your visit to Boston?" Daniel inquired.

Dr. West looked over his glasses at Daniel for a minute without replying. "Quite." The one word was like a period at the end of a sermon. Dr. West picked up his knife and fork and began eating his cold hotcakes, slowly, square by square.

"How is Mr. Blake?"

Dr. West consulted his watch. "Didn't see much of him."

His father was distinctly embarrassed. As if he were hiding a secret. As if he might really be part of a secret Tory committee, perhaps working with the governor just as Daniel had speculated on Derby Wharf. "Will you be going again soon?" he asked.

"One more trip and that will be the last."

It was such an unexpected answer, it took Daniel by surprise. One more trip, then what? Would his father take up his practice on a regular basis? Could they talk about Jeremy and Tillie and the addition to the house? One more trip—would that be for Tory business? Perhaps after word came from England?

"Hear any news in Boston?" Daniel inquired, watching his father closely. The very mention of Boston seemed to make his father uneasy.

"No. Nothing." Dr. West pushed his plate away from him and then as he glanced at Daniel, he apparently thought of something he could legitimately tell. "Only that the governor is coming to Salem the twenty-seventh of this month." He pushed his chair back. "To review the new Essex Regiment," he added as he stood up. "The governor and Secretary Flucker and General Brattle."

To Salem! Daniel grinned. The governor in Salem! The picture of what a great day it would be flashed through his mind—all the uniforms, the parading, the drumming, the gun firing, the fancy carriages, the important visitors.

"Did Governor Hutchison tell you? Did he tell you, himself?" Daniel asked.

His father was already on his way out of the room. Either he hadn't heard or he didn't choose to answer.

When Daniel stepped out of the house a few minutes later to go to school, the full force of spring hit him, just as it apparently was hitting the whole town. Up and down the street, doors were ajar and grown folks, not wearing any wraps at all, were standing by their front gates in awe—Jonathon Mansfield, the blacksmith, with a poker in his hand, John Morris, the saddlemaker, in his leather apron.

And the Widow Ray.

It was too late for Daniel to escape. She had already seen him and was walking in fast little steps into the street. "Well, Daniel West!" she cried. "I was just thinking about you." She turned and called to Peter over her shoulder. "Hurry up, Peter," she said. "Daniel's here to walk to school with you."

Daniel groaned. There was nothing to do but stand in the street and take the Widow Ray as if she were a dose of medicine souring up the day.

"Is your father back yet, dear?"

Dear!

Sensing she had said something wrong, the widow quickly dug into her apron pocket and brought out a handful of anise drops.

"I don't care for anise," Daniel said coldly.

The widow arched her eyebrows. "Well, you care for Indian pudding, I expect. I tell you what." Daniel gritted his teeth. "I'll send Peter over one night this week," she said, "with Indian pudding. You say your father's home?"

"Yes, he's home."

There was only so much medicine a person could stomach at one time and then Peter came rushing out with his schoolbooks and Daniel thought he'd about reached his quota. Setting off to school together, Daniel decided he'd just have to avoid looking at Peter. He didn't know what it was about the boy, but Peter was constantly reminding him of some form of mud life. Like thinking of Peter Ray's eyes when he saw the turtle. Nothing about Peter resembled any creature that had made it far enough up the ladder to be classified as a real animal. The way Peter attached himself to you, for instance. Exactly like one of his father's bloodletting leeches. And his lips. It was a disgusting thought, but Peter Ray's lips were as loose and elastic as two fishing worms.

Daniel was relieved when they reached the schoolyard and saw the other boys already assembled.

There were seven boys in Mr. Nicholl's school that Daniel and Beckett and Peter went to. It was a private school, specifically for boys who had finished at grammar school and were contemplating going on to study law or doctoring or the like at Harvard. It was a new school and because some of the fathers were not too pleased with what Mr. Nicholls had accomplished, it might not even last a second year. Dr. West had said that unless Daniel learned more than he had the first six months, he'd have to read privately with someone if he really decided to take the examinations for Harvard.

Politically, the boys in Daniel's class were almost equally divided—four Whigs and three Tories, not that anyone paid much attention to the difference. Benjie Stevens, for instance, the oldest in the group by over a year, was a Whig. And Charlie Putnam's father was on the Whigs' Committee of Correspondence, yet both these boys had always seen the seasons in and out with Daniel and Beckett, packing snowballs together, going after trout and chokeberries and clams and pigeon. Daniel couldn't see that England would ever need to come between them.

But Daniel wasn't thinking about Whigs and Tories when he stepped into the schoolyard. He was thinking how glad he was to get away from Peter Ray. He was thinking about how interested everyone would be in the news about the governor's coming.

He motioned for the boys to draw around. Then he told them. "Governor Hutchison," he said. "Secretary Flucker. General Brattle." It seemed to Daniel he could hear the fifes playing already and when he looked at Beckett, Daniel saw that Beckett could too.

But some of the others couldn't. Daniel didn't understand what was wrong until Benjie Stevens stepped apart from the group. He studied the sky a minute. Then he looked straight at Daniel.

"Governor Hutchison!" he said and he spat on the ground.

"Secretary Flucker!" Charlie Putnam said and he spat.

"General Brattle!" Thomas Cook was the one who spat now.

"That's supposed to be good news?" Benjie sneered. "The town crawling with Tories! I suppose the governor confided these happy tidings directly to your father?"

Daniel didn't know what made him answer as he did, except that he was mad. "I wouldn't be surprised," he snapped and, of course, he told himself, he wouldn't.

58

He didn't realize that what he'd done was to chalk another mark against his father's name. He didn't realize it until on the school steps, Benjie bowed low and swept his arm toward Daniel.

"And now, Lord West," he said, "won't you and your dear friend, the governor, come for *tea*? A nice cup of tea fresh from England!"

The boys went into the classroom and took their seats. The four Whigs lined up solidly on one side of the room—Benjie, Charlie, and the two Thomases, Thomas Cook and Thomas Clark. The three Tories took seats on the other side—Daniel, Beckett, and Peter Ray.

Benjie Stevens sent Daniel a note. *The next piece of news that comes to Salem,* he wrote, *the Whigs are going to get and get it first. And it better be more to their liking.*

Chapter Four

EVEN THOUGH it appeared that Charlie and Benjie were taking their politics more seriously than they had before, Daniel supposed that in a day or so they'd get off their high horse and be friends again. But day after day went by and the four Whigs maintained their solid line on one side of the classroom. Then one morning it became clear that they were not going to retreat.

Mr. Nicholls was giving a long-winded lecture on early Roman writers. He was like a bee, Mr. Nicholls. A drone, to be exact. He would fly from one topic to another, humming so monotonously no one bothered to follow his flight, and then all of a sudden he would land on a word and he would buzz. He would pick on a verb he had just used and without warning he would shout it out at some drowsing student and ask him to conjugate it. On this particular day he'd been mumbling along about a first-century Roman named Phaedrus who had said it was a good idea to submit to present evil for fear of attracting a greater one.

Then Mr. Nicholls landed on his word. "Submit!" he shouted. "Conjugate. Charles Putnam."

To Daniel's surprise Charlie seemed wide awake. He leaned over and looked straight at the Tories. Then he turned to Mr. Nicholls. "Sir," he said, "I am not acquainted with the word 'submit.' "

Right down the Whig line Mr. Nicholls went. Right down the Whig line the boys refused to conjugate. Benjie Stevens went further. He said that as far as he was concerned, the word "submit" had no past, present, or future. The only possible alternative for "submit," he said, was "resist" and he offered to conjugate that. Sizing up the temper of the four boys, Mr. Nicholls accepted the offer.

After the noon meal that day the Whigs came back to school, each with a large R for "resist" chalked on the front of his Latin book. At the end of school the Whigs divided. Charlie and Benjie walked out to Salem Neck, where incoming ships could first be spotted; the other two took a station at a strategic point where riders might pass with word from Boston. Obviously they were determined to be the first to get the king's news.

"Well, let them," Daniel said. "Who cares? Besides, the news may come another way entirely. After all, it was through my father we heard about the governor's visit. And my father says he's going to Boston again."

Meanwhile, however, with the Whigs in Mr. Nicholls' class so well organized, it seemed to Beckett and Daniel downright lazy to be doing nothing. Especially now that they had had their eyes opened about the governor's visit. They had known, of course, that the governor was not liked by Whigs, but he was due to leave soon and would be replaced by a new governor. They hadn't supposed a man in his last days of office would arouse so much spite. And after all, a review was a review. The parades and marching would be like nothing Salem had seen for a long time. Did a person have to *like* the fifer these days, Daniel wondered, before he could enjoy the music?

It was only four days now until the governor's arrival and Daniel and Beckett, sitting in Daniel's kitchen, shelling the last of the winter's supply of hickory nuts, were trying to think of some way they could offset Whig rudeness to the governor if it came to that, some way to show the governor that there were young folks in town who considered his visit an honor. It was a good time to make such plans; Daniel and Beckett were alone. Dr. West had gone up to Danvers on a sick call and would be away all evening; Hannah had taken Sarah to visit Jonathon.

Beckett threw a hickory shell into the hearth. "Maybe we could put placards on our gateposts," he said. "The Tory gateposts. We could say 'Welcome, Governor,' or some such thing."

Daniel shook his head. "All the houses that didn't have placards would stick out. Just as if they said, 'You're *not* welcome, Governor.' "

Beckett sighed. "Yes, and there are more Whig homes in Salem now than loyal ones."

"Well, you know what men do when they want to pay their respects?"

"What?"

"They write a letter," Daniel said. "An address is what they call it."

It didn't seem like a very exciting idea. When a person really wanted to blow a bugle, when he really wanted to tie up all the Whigs in town and hide them for a day, writing a letter was a poor substitute. It seemed, however, the most practical one.

Daniel and Beckett finished off the nuts, brushed their laps free of crumbs, and went into Dr. West's office for paper and pen. By the time they settled themselves at the kitchen table, they had decided that they would write and sign the letter now but not go after other signatures until the governor had arrived. If word got around among Whig boys that young Tories were making an address, it might stimulate them to mischief they hadn't considered.

Beckett persuaded Daniel to do the actual writing because he was better at the flourishes. The way Daniel elaborated on the tail of a *y*, Beckett claimed, would give tone to any letter. So Daniel began:

May it please your Excellency, he wrote. Three *y*'s on the first line!

Beckett moved a lamp to the table, trying out phrases and wording while he walked about. Daniel's pen made small scratching noises, stopped, started, stopped again. Then Daniel read aloud the first sentence:

"We, the undersigned, who are under age and therefore not able to participate in official acts of greeting, beg leave to present you with our dutiful respects on the occasion of your visit to Salem."

The two boys grinned. It might not be blowing a bugle, they agreed, but it came close. When you found the right words and rolled them out in style, it was like unfurling a carpet. When they came to the closing, Daniel wrote: *We are, your Excellency, your most humble and obedient servants.*

They were admiring their work and blowing on the ink when the back door opened. Daniel supposed it would be Hannah and Sarah but instead Peter Ray walked in.

The first thing that Daniel noticed about Peter was that he was carrying an Indian pudding. The second thing he noticed was that Peter was smiling, obviously delighted to find the two boys together, obviously anticipating a little visit. The third thing he noticed and he wished he hadn't was that Peter Ray had a cold; his nose was running.

Daniel and Beckett jumped to their feet, standing before the table so the letter couldn't be seen.

"Why, thank you, Peter," Daniel said, taking the pudding before Peter could properly offer it.

"Your father likes Indian pudding," Peter said. "My mother knows all the things your father likes."

Daniel grunted. He put a hand on Peter's elbow and tried guiding him to the door. "Thank your mother," he said gruffly.

But Peter wouldn't be guided. "I don't have to go yet," he said. "I can stay and visit. What are you boys doing anyway?"

"Nothing." Beckett had his arms akimbo, hiding most of the table.

"Come on. Let me stay." Peter held on to the back of a chair as if he expected to be pushed out of the room. "We're good friends." He hesitated. "Please."

Daniel knew he should feel sorry for a turtle with its neck sticking out so far, but he didn't. All he wanted to do was to poke the stick through the slats again.

"For heaven's sakes, Peter," he said, "why don't you blow your nose?"

Meekly Peter took out his handkerchief, one end of which had been made into a knotty with a small stone inside for swinging at the heads of younger boys. The heavy knotty didn't leave much room for blowing. In fact, it made the whole process so complicated and revolting that Daniel and Beckett both turned their heads aside, waiting until it was over.

They were off guard only a moment but that was all Peter needed. In four quick steps he had dodged Daniel and was behind Beckett; he was standing over the table, looking down at the letter.

May it please your Excellency. He made a sucking noise as he read. When he looked up, there was a spot of cunning in the center of each eye, a kind of cunning, Daniel thought, peculiar to reptiles. "Why didn't you tell me you were writing to the governor?" he asked. "I'm a Tory."

There was, of course, no point trying to conceal anything now.

"We were going to tell you," Daniel sighed. "Later. We didn't want anyone to know yet."

Peter read the letter through. "Can I sign?"

Daniel stalled for time. He said it required a conference and he and Beckett stepped to the other side of the room. It would be a shame, they agreed, to have Peter Ray's muddy little signature on that beautiful piece of paper—at least tonight. Especially the third name from the top. Later, of course, they'd want every signature they could get, but now they had to find some way to keep Peter from telling about the letter until they were ready.

It took only a few minutes to make an appropriate plan. They crossed back to Peter.

"It's this way," Beckett said. "We have to be careful. We don't want anyone to sign who hasn't proved his loyalty."

"You know I'm loyal," Peter said.

"Then you won't mind proving it. We just don't want to be embarrassed later by any timid Tories." Beckett looked very important. "We think everyone who signs our letter should pass a little test."

Peter wet his lips. "What kind of test?"

"We'll show you. We'll take you out now and give it to you if you like."

"Then can I sign?"

"Not tonight. If you pass the test, you can sign your name when we get the other signatures. You can even be high on the list. That is, of course, if up to that time you haven't told about it."

Beckett folded the letter carefully and put it in the top drawer of the china cabinet where the Wests kept their company silver. Daniel went down to the cellar. When he came back he was carrying a toy sword he'd made years ago out of two pieces of wood lashed together. The tip of the sword had been whittled to a sharp point.

"All ready," he said. "Let's go."

As soon as he stepped outside, Daniel was glad that he wasn't in Peter Ray's shoes. It was a still night lighted by a badly shaped moon, one of those nights when the water in the harbor was glassy and when the reflections in the water seemed more real than the objects they were reflecting. The shadows on the street were like those reflections, each with a life of its own. As the three boys walked, their lanterns in their right hands, their shadows veered off to the left, elongated people on the ground who might at any moment rise up and take the place of the boys and turn them into black nothings instead. For a long time they didn't talk. They went past the Sign of the Gilt Bible where the bookseller lived; they crossed Marblehead Road; they came to the black Witch House where Judge Corwen had lived, where in the old days witches had been questioned. In the middle of the street was the well the witches had drunk from. The three boys and the three shadows swung to the left of the well.

It was not until they were in open country that Peter spoke.

"Where are we going?" he asked.

Beckett explained it all very matter-of-factly as if it were not uncommon for people to set out at night for Gallows Hill where the witches had been hung. The way he told it, it was a simple matter to go alone to the top of the hill, brandish the wooden sword and swear allegiance to the king—loudly, of course, so Beckett and Daniel could hear at the bottom of the hill, and then plunge the sword into the grave of a witch.

"Into a grave?" Peter whispered.

"Yep. Into a grave." Beckett didn't slow his footsteps a whit.

They were in Blubber Hollow now and Gallows Hill rose ahead of them, not a very big hill nor with much cover on it. It was raw-looking, stony and still, with only a few trees at the top near the graves. Black,

winter-loving locusts they were, as bare now as they
were in the dead of cold, and the shadows they threw
were fragments of themselves—fingers and arms here
and there, bones scattered over the hillside.

Peter stopped. He put his hand on Daniel's arm.
"If I do that," he said, "will you tell your father?"

Daniel stared straight ahead. "Tell him what?"

Peter's hand tightened. His voice lowered. "Tell
him something nice about me." He hesitated. "And
about my mother," he whispered.

Daniel shivered. It was as if he'd touched the under-
side, the soft, wet belly of a turtle with his bare hand.
He cleared his throat. "If you're a loyal Tory," he
said shortly, "I'll tell him so."

Daniel handed Peter the sword and Beckett coached
him in the exact words he should use.

"Can't I just pledge allegiance?" Peter begged.

Beckett shook his head. The wording, he said, was
important. The exact wording. He made Peter repeat
the pledge again.

Then Daniel and Beckett watched Peter inch his
way slowly up the hill, his lantern flickering in one
hand, the toy sword dangling from the other. When
he'd gone some distance, Daniel and Beckett put their
lanterns on the ground; quickly and quietly they
circled the hill, climbing it from another side; then
they lay down on their stomachs where they could
watch Peter perform.

Peter was so long in coming that at first they thought
he had turned tail but then they realized he was only

slow, for which, Daniel conceded, he could hardly be blamed. They heard him before they saw him. He took a few steps, stopped, panted and sniffled back his cold, then he took a few more steps, panted and sniffled again. His whole progress had a wet sound, as if it were a swamp and not a hill he was traversing. When he got to the top, he raised one foot, then the other, apparently wishing there were some place other than the ground to set them. After a moment he put down his lantern. The light from the lantern showed that he was standing directly before a mound of earth, obviously a grave. He jumped back. He stood for a moment looking at the grave and then he gave an enormous sniff. He raised his toy sword a few inches in the air and waggled it.

"I, Peter Ray, do hereby swear allegiance to George the Third, King of England and America." His voice was loud enough. Shrill even. "I swear to defend the King with my blood." He made a choking sound. "To the last breath of my life if I am called upon to do so."

Daniel stirred uncomfortably on the ground. He realized he hadn't looked to see if he was lying on a grave or not.

Beckett poked him. "You see any witches?" he whispered.

"Not yet. You?"

"No, but I bet they're all over."

Daniel knew it wouldn't take much to make him see a witch. Nor the ghosts of the onlookers, either. They were almost the worst, Daniel thought—all those

70

people who had poured out of Salem to see the hang-
ings. Right on this very hillside they had jostled and
pushed each other for a better view. Without blinking
they had watched the witches hang from their ropes,
waiting until they were dead, dead, dead.

Daniel closed his eyes. He couldn't look at Peter any
longer. It was hard even to listen. Peter's voice had
weakened. He was whimpering now.

"And I swear not to divulge any secrets in my posses-
sion. And let anyone who hears me, living . . . or dead,
say me nay."

It was at this point that Beckett and Daniel had
planned to wail out a few unearthly "nays" from their
hiding place, but Daniel couldn't do it.

He put his hand on Beckett's arm. "I've had
enough," he whispered. "How about you?"

"Yea."

The two boys stood up. Daniel spoke as naturally
as he could so the sound of a voice wouldn't undo Peter
altogether.

"We're right here, Peter. You did fine," he said.
"You don't have to put the sword in the grave if you
don't want to."

Peter seemed to shrivel up for a moment and then
when he realized his ordeal was over, he wiped his
sleeve across his nose and made a scraping noise that
was supposed to be a laugh.

"When the time comes," Daniel said, "your name
can be third on the letter." They were walking down
the hill now and Daniel was trying hard not to wonder

what it would be like to spend a whole life being Peter Ray. A whole life! "If you're third signer," he said suddenly, "the governor will know that among Tory boys, you're a leader."

As soon as he'd spoken, he knew he'd made a mistake. Almost immediately he could feel a change in Peter's gait. In the space of a few minutes Peter worked himself up from a shuffle to a walk; then he improved on his step until he reached a full-fledged strut. "I guess you know now," he said, "it takes more than a few witches to scare me." He nudged Daniel, like one turtle to another. "I guess you can tell your father, Daniel, that if I were around all the time, I'd be someone he could take pride in."

It was as if Peter had taken a ramrod and rammed it into a musket full of powder and the musket was Daniel's. "You leave my father out of this!" Daniel shouted. "You and your mother, you leave him alone!" In a moment he quieted. "I'll tell my father what I said I'd tell him," he said, "and no more. And I don't want to hear any more about it."

Without further conversation the three boys walked to Peter's house. They dropped Peter off but even then they didn't take up speaking for a while.

It was Beckett who broke the silence. He didn't look at Daniel; he seemed to be studying the moon.

"It's been a busy evening," he said.

"Yea," Daniel agreed.

"Full of ups and downs."

"Yea."

72

"We got the letter to the governor written."

"Yep."

"And we fixed Peter Ray. He won't tell about it."

"Guess not."

"All in all, we advanced the Tory cause."

"Guess so."

Beckett pushed his hat back on his head. "Seems as if we deserve a little reward."

For the first time Daniel looked at Beckett. "What have you got in mind?"

"Well," Beckett said, "I was just thinking. Seems as if tonight's a good night. How about a cup of tea?"

Daniel grinned. "Sounds like an excellent idea."

When they got back to the West house, Daniel checked and found Hannah and Sarah had come home and were in bed. Dr. West was not in the house but he'd be no danger, Daniel pointed out. They'd hear him in plenty of time to hide the evidence. The noise of the horse going to the stable would be their warning and it always took Dr. West twenty minutes to half an hour to bed the horse down for the night.

Beckett built up the fire in the hearth and hung the teakettle over it. Daniel got out two cups from the cupboard and reached down the white china teapot that hadn't been used since long before his mother's death. He felt a sudden flash of despair, remembering how his mother would sometimes touch the teapot, almost apologetically, as it sat neglected on the shelf. He was used to these flashes. Grief, he had discovered, consisted of wells and potholes hidden under the surface of a day; a person never knew when he was going to step into one.

"What about the Indian pudding?" Beckett asked. "Would that be a good accompaniment?"

Daniel set the teapot on the table, took a deep breath, and said the Indian pudding would be a very good accompaniment. In fact, he added, it would be a fine idea to finish it off before his father came home. The less Dr. West was exposed to the Widow Ray's cooking, the better.

Together Daniel and Beckett went up to the pie room for the tin of tea. While they were still there, they took the lid off for a sniff. Just to make it more tantalizing, Beckett said.

They took several sniffs. Then Beckett put his head to one side as he considered how best to describe the smell.

"Not tantalizing," he said.

"What then?"

"Intoxicating," Beckett decided. "Unquestionably intoxicating."

They were both laughing as they came downstairs, bumping into each other, skipping steps in their haste. Daniel was carrying the tin, hugging it in both arms in front of him, and Beckett was grabbing for it; they were trying to outdo each other in foolishness and horseplay as they stumbled into the kitchen.

And there was Dr. West. He was still carrying his doctor's case. He looked at the two boys and the tin of tea in Daniel's arms. It was a moment when Daniel should either have kept quiet or have said exactly the right thing, if there was a right thing to say. He did neither.

"How did you get home?" he blurted. "I didn't hear you."

"That's quite obvious." Dr. West set down his case. "Apparently I got home before you did and was in the stable taking care of the horse when you came. Now it's my turn for questions," he said. "Well?"

Daniel put the tea on the table. He didn't know where or how to begin. His father didn't make it any easier. It was the first time in months that *all* of his father seemed to be here, all of him listening, not part of him off by himself where he couldn't hear. His father took off his hat. He didn't walk over to the hook in that deliberate way he'd developed and hang his hat as if there were only one way to hang a hat. He simply flipped it toward the hook, not looking to see if it landed right or not.

"Well?" he repeated.

Daniel began with the night of Judge Ropes' death. He watched his father's face to see the anger build up as he went on with the story. He even told about Mr. Allison and how everyone knew about the tea. He told about the letter to Governor Hutchison, but it wasn't until he had Peter Ray up Gallows Hill that he noticed that his father didn't seem too terribly angry, after all. His face, which had been so tight and tired, seemed actually to loosen up as Daniel described Peter jumping back from the witch's grave, adding, as he felt obliged to, that he supposed Peter was, if nothing else, a loyal Tory. Then Daniel took a deep breath.

"After that," he said, "Beckett and I felt a little stimulant was in order."

Dr. West was sitting in the rocking chair now. He reared back and held the chair on the hind end of the rockers. "So that's the tale?" he said.

Daniel nodded. "I'll put the tea back where it came from," he said. "I won't touch it again."

Dr. West rocked forward. "I wouldn't do that," he said quietly. He pointed to the table, where the teapot and cups were waiting. "As long as you've got things set up," he said, "why don't you get down another cup? We'll all have a little stimulant."

Daniel let out a sigh. It was as if for a long time someone had been holding down his springs and had finally let go. He leaped to the china cupboard. Beckett, making loud, appreciative noises, spooned the tea into the teapot and poured in the steaming water. While the tea steeped, Daniel dished out the Indian pudding. He felt no call to mention where it had come from.

As they took chairs around the table, Dr. West chuckled. "So you got Peter Ray up Gallows Hill, did you?"

They took their first lingering sip of tea. It was delicious, of course—more so than it had ever been when it was the regular accompaniment to every meal. Still, it wasn't the tea that was important. Daniel couldn't keep his eyes off his father, so miraculously returned to his former self, tipping back his chair, telling stories of his own youth, recalling escapades,

76

just as he'd done in the old days. They'd all sat around the fire then, his mother at the center of the conversation as she'd been at the center of everything, laughing at his father's stories, encouraging him to come out of his natural quietness—a happy quietness in those times, not like the quietness that hung now like a stone around his father's neck.

If only the evening didn't have to end, Daniel thought. If only he could keep it going, the way a person keeps a soft ball up in the air, running under it and hitting it, running under so it won't fall to the ground.

"If the news from London is favorable," Daniel said, "maybe we can have tea all the time."

"Maybe." Dr. West sighed. "Peace would be wonderful." The curtain came down on his face. "That's all I want now," he said. "Peace." He got up and went to the window. When he turned around, what he said didn't seem to follow. "I'm going to Boston tomorrow," he said. He looked at Daniel as if he wanted to say more. In fact, he even began. "Daniel—" but then he stopped as if there was a wall and he couldn't speak through it.

"I'll be taking the chaise this time," he said.

Dr. West had always gone on horseback. He wouldn't take the chaise unless he were going to bring someone back. Daniel's mind raced. There would be a lot of strangers coming to Salem for the review, important Tories who would be needing transportation one way or another.

"You'll be back in time for the governor's review?" he asked.

Dr. West nodded. "Oh yes, I'll be back in time for that." He went to the lamp and adjusted the wick so the flame wouldn't burn too high.

The evening was over.

Chapter Five

Among Mr. Nicholls' many defects he had one
quality that the boys in his class agreed was
admirable, and that was his poor health. Mr. Nicholls
had a wheezing sickness that came on miraculously in
the spring and fall just when the weather was at its
best. He claimed his sickness had something to do with

79

the change of seasons but the boys took personal credit. It just showed, they said, what prayer could do when people really put their minds to it. As soon as they saw the sheet of paper on the school door indicating Mr. Nicholls' absence, they would let out a whoop. "Libera!" they would cry and take off for the river or the shore. It was the only word in the Latin language, Daniel thought, that was an improvement on English. The translation was "free men, free to do as they will," but it was not only the meaning but the sound of the word that the boys liked. "Libera"—it had the ring of sudden freedom, of deliverance, of triumph; it was exactly the word a person needed when he was let out of school unexpectedly.

Daniel thought it was probably too much to hope for a vacation during the week of the governor's review, but as he approached school the day before, he could see that familiar sheet of paper on the school door. Charlie Putnam was standing before it, grinning.

"Libera!" Daniel called out and ran up the steps to make sure the paper said what it should. It did. *Mr. Nicholls is ill,* it said, *and will be unable to conduct classes for the next week.* Below this was the week's assignment.

Daniel glanced at Charlie; he had stopped grinning but Daniel pretended not to notice. "The river or the shore?" he asked, trying to make his voice sound as if nothing had ever come between them. After all, if anything could cut across their differences, it should be a vacation. "How about the river?"

80

Down the street other boys were approaching, Benjie on one side, Beckett on the other.

"I'm going out to the Neck," Charlie said shortly. His head was lowered. "Benjie will come with me. And the Thomases." Suddenly he turned to Daniel. "I can't do anything with you, Daniel," he said. "We made a pact."

"A pact?"

"The Whig boys did. Not to be friends with the Tories until the news comes. And then not unless it turns out right."

"You act as if we didn't both want the same thing. Nothing would please me more than to have the tea tax repealed."

"You are a friend to the governor," Charlie said. "You're a submitter. If the tax isn't repealed, you'll go along with it."

"So?" Daniel snapped back. "We can differ. That's what freedom is, isn't it? Freedom to differ."

Charlie turned on his heel. "Either you're with us or you're against us," he said. He ran down the steps to meet Benjie. "Libera!" he cried.

Beckett joined Daniel on the school steps and together they watched Benjie and Charlie set off for the Neck. It was the first surprise holiday the boys hadn't taken off together.

"Well," Beckett said at last, "if that's the way it's going to be, let's go."

"Might as well." Daniel kicked at a stone in the road. What kind of freedom was it, he asked himself,

81

that didn't allow for difference of opinion? All the Whigs wanted was freedom to do things *their* way. They were no better than Parliament.

Without having discussed it, Daniel and Beckett were headed for the river. Daniel knew that Beckett's father was taking their sloop out of the water today for its yearly tarring. Beckett would certainly want to see how he was making out.

"You'll likely want to stay and help with the boat, Beckett," he said.

"Maybe for a while," Beckett agreed. "You wouldn't mind for a while, would you?"

"No reason you can't stay all day if you want to." If it were his boat, Daniel thought, he'd certainly want to stay now that the opportunity presented itself, but Beckett said no, there was all week to help and on the first day of a holiday he wanted to be with Daniel.

They had reached the part of town now where the river smell took over and the town smell stopped. Daniel had often thought that if he were dropped down blindfolded on the North River, he'd know where he was. Even though they were so near the mouth of the river where the fresh and salt water met, the river had its own distinctive smell, flat and almost metallic; a working smell, Daniel thought, as compared to the free, fresh smell of the ocean. If he were blindfolded, he'd even know what side of the bridge he was on. The eastern side smelled of fish from the flake yards where the cod was set out to dry and the western side smelled sweet from Major Sprague's distillery.

Beckett's father had drawn the boat up on the western side. The masts were out and the boat was turned over so he could scrape off the barnacles that had accumulated during the winter. Mr. Foote glanced up as the boys approached. Although he was a lawyer, he looked as if he had been built for the outdoors, a square-faced, square-shouldered man who, contrary to the normal practice and except for dress occasions, wore his own hair plaited in the back instead of wearing a wig.

"Not skipping school, are you?" Mr. Foote asked.

"No. Mr. Nicholls is sick." Beckett went on to explain about the Whig boys taking off by themselves.

Mr. Foote shook his head. "Well, if you've got nothing better to do," he said, "you can lend a hand for a while."

Mr. Foote had only one extra scraper and he tossed it to Beckett, adding that Daniel could take a turn whenever he wanted. But Daniel didn't want to, not that he'd object to the work but he sensed the satisfaction it would give a person to scrape the barnacles off his own boat and watch the wood come clean. As Beckett and his father scraped, Daniel circled the boat, admiring the lines, the sturdiness, the curving of the sides as they came together sharply to form the bow, a boat shaped to ride out storms and at the same time to take advantage of fair weather and calm seas. It was just the right size too, Daniel thought—small enough for one man to handle, big enough to hold a party of eight or more. As much as Daniel admired the boat, however, he knew that not having a boat of his own, he didn't look at it in the same way as Beckett did. Daniel looked at it as an outsider, as a man who longs for a horse looks at another man's horse, appreciatively but holding back the full force of his admiration, that total feeling that comes only with owning.

He looked down at the name of the boat painted in black on the side. The letters were upside down and faded from the winter's weathering but he knew them well enough—*Allegiance*—and there was a small crown painted above them.

"You folks going to keep the name," Daniel asked, "or are you going to change it? You meet up with a Whig sloop someday and you may run into trouble."

"We're going to paint it blacker than ever." Mr. Foote smiled. "I've got some soot and lampblack I've been saving. Might even make the crown a little bigger."

Daniel grinned. That was one of the nice qualities about the Footes, he thought. They didn't backtrack. They said what they thought and did what they believed and that was that.

There were other nice qualities, too. Daniel liked to watch them work together, each one sensing what the other needed without having to ask or correct or give instructions. Talking about work, Daniel always thought, was what made work tedious, the constant back and forth that some people indulged in about how a job should be done, this way and not that way, this first and then that, faster or slower, me or you. The

Foote men just did the work and talked about other things. They planned fishing trips, they talked of the review, they joked and teased each other. Daniel entered into the talk and laughter until all at once as he looked at Beckett and Mr. Foote, he felt as he had when he had stood admiring the boat, holding back, enjoying something that wasn't his—a certain light-heartedness between father and son might never be his again. He stepped away from the boat.

"I guess I'll go over to Jeremy's," he said to Beckett, "while you scrape."

"Well, I'll stop after a bit," Beckett said, "and I'll come over there and pick you up. We'll go to the country."

"You just go on scraping," Daniel said, "as long as you've a mind to. I may go home from Jeremy's. My father said he'd be home in time for the review. Likely he'll be coming in this afternoon. Let's go to the country another day, Beckett." He looked up at the sky. "It looks as though we may have rain by afternoon anyway."

Jeremy's house was on the fish side of the bridge but far enough away from the flake yards that it didn't get the smell unless the wind was blowing just right, and for those times Tillie kept a pile of lightwood knots handy for the fire, those resinous pieces of yellow pine that make a whole house smell like a pinewoods.

The house didn't smell of pine today, however; it smelled of cedar. Tillie was ironing. Her board was set across the back of two chairs and on one end of the board was a spray of cedar. Every once in a while Tillie would run her iron over the green spray and the juice from the spray would make her iron run smooth. The room was spread with clothing, unironed pieces filling the chairs, shirts hanging on chair backs, Jonathon's clothes covering the top of the chest and suspended from drawer knobs. Jeremy was sitting carefully on a chair before the table, leaning forward so he wouldn't muss the shirt hanging at his back while he worked with an assortment of the heavy wire he used to make fishhooks. Jonathon was asleep in his crib.

"You're just in time," Tillie said as Daniel stepped into the room. "You can help me fold this sheet."

Daniel went to the ironing board, took two corners of Tillie's sheet while she took the other two and they backed away from each other until the sheet was taut. Tillie gave it a few flaps and then they began folding, bringing the corners together one way and then another, walking toward each other, then separating, as if they were performing a dance step. When it was finished, Tillie put it on one of the chairs that held the ironing board.

"That's the end of the sheets," she said. She lifted a hot iron from the hearth and ran it, sizzling, over the cedar spray.

Daniel sat down beside Jeremy, watching him sharpen the point of a hook, but he felt restless. Wherever he went, everyone was busy with his own work.

"What time is it, Jeremy?" he asked.

Jeremy put down his knife and took his big watch out of his pocket. "Eleven o'clock."

It was probably too early for his father to be back, but Daniel was thinking maybe he'd go home anyway, when a knock came at the door. Immediately afterward the door opened and Hannah walked in. She looked around and spotted Daniel, then she simply stood in the doorway, staring at the room. When she recovered herself, she looked first at Tillie and then at Jeremy, trying, it seemed, to send them a message without needing to speak.

Tillie put the iron down on the trivet. "Where's Sarah?" she said. "Has something happened to Sarah?"

Hannah shook her head. "No. Sarah's all right. She's home." She paused a moment. "Home with her father."

Daniel grinned. "He's back, is he?"

"Yes, he's back," but Hannah was still shaking her head, almost as if she were telling Daniel not to smile, not to jump to conclusions. She took a step toward him, but then she stopped and, her hands dangling at her sides, she made an announcement to the room at large, not looking at anybody.

"He's back, all right," she said. "And he's brought home a wife." She went on as if she were repeating a lesson. "He brought her in about an hour ago, introduced her, and we showed her the house and then he said, 'Go fetch Daniel wherever he is. I want him to meet his new mother.'"

"No!" Daniel jumped to his feet, knocking the chair over behind him, sending one of Jeremy's freshly

ironed shirts sprawling on the floor. "No!" His head
pounded with the word "No," his heart hammered
"No," his feet stamped "No" as he began pacing the
room, as if by shouting loud enough and walking fast
enough, he could deny the "Yes" he saw written miser-
ably across the faces of Jeremy and Tillie and Hannah.

Jeremy snapped his knife shut. "Did your father give
you no inkling, lad?" he asked quietly.

"No."

"I guess that's why he's been in Boston so much."

"No! He's been doing Tory business."

Jeremy sighed. "You just guessed that. You never
knew it. But it will be all right, boy. It will work out."

Daniel slumped into his chair. With one part of his
mind he knew what Jeremy was doing. He was trying
to pour oil on the heaving waters that had swept into
the room, but Daniel didn't want any oil. All he
wanted was to go back to the moment before Hannah
had come in. Then let her come in, if she had to, and
borrow a fresh egg. Or let her come in and show off
some new shells. Or let her come in and scold him for
not bringing in the water that morning. Or let her
not come in at all, Daniel thought. Just go away and
not come in at all.

"Take your time, lad," Jeremy was saying softly.
"You'll get your wind back in a minute. Maybe it's the
best thing. Your house has been without a captain and
mate long enough."

"No," Daniel repeated. It was all he could say.

Tillie couldn't say anything. She slipped from the

ironing board over to the crib. Heavily she stooped over, picked up Jonathon, then sat down in the rocker. Holding him in her arms, she rocked back and forth, back and forth—not steady rocking but rocking by fits and starts as if she were trying to keep her balance on top of the waves.

After a while Jeremy spoke again. "Don't hurry, Daniel," he said, "but sooner or later you'll have to go. And no matter how you feel, you'll have to put a good face on it."

"Your father's expecting you for the noon meal, Daniel." Hannah was standing at the door, still talking in a reading voice. "I'm not to serve dinner in the kitchen any more. She gave me instructions. In the dining room, she said. And company silver every day. And she has a bell she'll ring from the table when she wants me. A bell," she repeated. "And dinner's to be at twelve-thirty sharp."

Daniel didn't want to hear any more. "All right," he said. "All right. I'll go." He dropped his voice to a whisper. "I'm not ready but I'll go."

He stepped briefly behind Tillie's chair and put his hand on her shoulder and then he walked out of the house with Hannah behind him. He didn't look back at Jonathon or at Jeremy or at Tillie or at the room he'd come to love so much. All the way home he walked as if he were sleepwalking, past the saddler's and the blacksmith's, all the way up the front steps of his house, opening the door as if it were someone else's door and he were a stranger.

She was in the dining room looking at his mother's yellow fruit plates and Sarah was holding her hand. As soon as Sarah saw Daniel, she broke away and began dancing. "We've got a new mother, Daniel!" she sang. "We've got a new mother!"

Sarah didn't seem real. She was part of the whole nightmare and when Daniel's father came in and hushed Sarah and made the proper introductions, he became a character in the nightmare too.

"I know this comes as a surprise, Daniel," Dr. West said, "but I decided it was better this way. This is your new mother."

There could be no right words for anything that was so wrong, and no matter what anyone said, it only sent Daniel deeper into his nightmare. He heard himself mumbling words, but surely it wasn't he, Daniel West, acknowledging this woman, accepting her presence—a person he couldn't even bring himself to look at. He concentrated on a spot over her right shoulder, looking out the window at the pump in the backyard, that reliable old pump that had brought water up out of the ground year in and year out, in the dryest of seasons, for as long as he could remember.

He kept looking back at the pump off and on during the noon meal over which *she* presided, sitting in his mother's chair, directing her conversation first to one and then another, as if she were dispensing gifts. Daniel spoke only when necessary. His nightmare was suddenly taking on a new dimension. While most of his mind was tumbling about in that blurred region where dreams take place, one corner of his mind had become extraordinarily alert. It was as if he were lost in a dark forest and yet able to shoot a gun and have it hit squarely on his target. When *she* commented how nice it was going to be to have a son studying law at Harvard, that alert part of his mind pulled a trigger. "She's a deciding woman," it said, and he steeled himself against it. When she told Sarah about the clothes and manner of the ladies in Boston, the gun went off again. "She's a woman who puts on airs," and he determined to resist her. When she described some of her household belongings that would be arriving by wagon the next day, there was another shot. "She has money," and he decided never to use it. When she began talking about her good friend, Daniel Leonard, a representative to the General Court, Daniel looked at her for the first time. At least she was a Tory.

He didn't know what he expected to see when he finally looked in her face. Not a Widow Ray; he knew better than that. A Boston lady, he supposed that's what you'd call her. Her hair piled up high. Powdered. The gun went off in a series of quick shots. Sharp eyes. Pointed chin. A long neck. She wasn't a person who was going to warm this house. She was simply going to be here day after day, interfering and ordering. Meal after meal, he'd be pinned at this dining room table while *she* rang that little silver bell at her right hand for Hannah to do her bidding.

"I think I'll go down to the river and help Beckett with his boat this afternoon," he said suddenly, wondering why he had spoken aloud.

She was ringing her bell. When Hannah ran in from

the kitchen, she smiled sweetly. "More bread, please."
Then she turned to Daniel, retaining the same smile
she'd used on Hannah.

"If your teacher's sick," she said, "I expect he left
you an assignment, didn't he?"

"Yes, ma'am. I have all week to do it."

"Well, I know boys." She laughed. "I had a brother
when I was growing. And I know a boy has to be held
to the mark else he goes wild." She waggled a finger
at Daniel. "And unless he studies, he won't pass any
Harvard examinations."

"I have never said for certain I am going to
Harvard."

"Oh, of course, you are." She laughed again. Her
voice was like a bell tinkling.

Daniel was not going to argue today, nor was he
going to obey nor was he going to resist. He glanced at
his father. Dr. West was spreading a slice of bread with
apple butter, taking his knife and smoothing the butter
down again and again, then carefully going around the
edges to make sure none had dribbled off.

"When is Jonathon coming home?" Daniel asked.

Dr. West looked up. "In a couple of weeks," he said.
"After your new mother has had a chance to get
acquainted, after she has fixed things to her liking."

After dinner *she* went upstairs to take a rest and
Sarah tagged along after her. Dr. West went out on a
sick call and Hannah went into the kitchen. But
Daniel just went on sitting at the table, watching
Hannah come and go as she cleared, listening to her

92

in the kitchen as she washed up. Then her footsteps went off in the direction of her bedroom.

Still Daniel didn't move. He stared out the window at the pump and at the spring grass that thrust itself up between the cracks of the pump platform. He looked at the sky, noting how dark it had become. A storm was definitely on its way and he waited for it. When it came, it was a sudden downpour, flattening the grass in the platform cracks, streaming through the hawthorn tree, drumming on the windowpane.

Sometime during the storm Daniel was aware of footsteps in the kitchen again. He supposed that Hannah, unable to rest, had come back to make sure she'd left everything to *her* liking. He pushed himself away from the table. He wanted to talk now and the only person in the house to talk to was Hannah.

But when he opened the door, he saw that it wasn't Hannah who was there. It was Peter Ray. He was standing on the rag rug, dripping, his hair matted down like something washed up from the riverbank.

"You're forever bursting in here," Daniel said coldly. "I didn't hear you knock."

"It was raining too hard. I didn't take the time."

"You've been here quite a while. I heard your footsteps." Pools of water lay all over the kitchen floor. "What did you come for anyway?"

"I came to find out if it was true," Peter said. "Some people told me and I didn't believe it."

"What?"

Peter stared at the floor. "Well," he said, "I know it

93

can't be so or you would have told me long ago. But Mr. Mansfield saw your father come into town and he said your father had brought home a wife."

"He did bring home a wife."

Slowly Peter raised his head. His eyes held a hatred that looked as if it had been rotting in a stagnant place for a long time. "Why didn't you tell me?" he snarled. "You knew what I was hoping for! And Mr. Mansfield —you know what he did? He *laughed* when he told me."

Daniel walked over to the window. He certainly wasn't going to admit to Peter Ray that Dr. West's own son hadn't known either. "It was not your affair," he snapped. "And it isn't your affair now. Just get out."

"With pleasure," Peter hissed. "But you'll be sorry, Daniel West. You'll be sorry." He slammed the kitchen door.

Daniel found an old cloth of Hannah's and got down on his hands and knees to mop up after Peter, scrubbing as if he'd like to go right through the floorboards.

Sarah came in and stood behind him. "You know what, Daniel?" she said. "She's going to make me a pink silk dress. *Silk.*"

"Let her. Let her make you two silk dresses for all I care." Daniel took the cloth to the back door and wrung it out.

Sarah pulled at his sleeve. "Daniel," she whispered, "Daniel—don't be mad, Daniel."

He looked down at his sister. He supposed she'd been struggling in her own way, running back and forth to the Widow Ray's, filling herself up on anise drops. He put his hand on her head. "You be glad if you want to, Sarah," he sighed. "Only don't tell me what to be. I don't want anyone telling me what to be or not to be."

Chapter Six

THE NEXT MORNING there was a Liberty Gift on
Daniel's front doorstep. The new Mrs. West was
the one who discovered it. Her nose was puckered as
she swept into the kitchen for breakfast. "Something
is spoiled in this kitchen," she said coldly. "I smelled
it all the way up in my bedroom."

Hannah straightened up from the fireplace. She was

wearing a starched white apron that Daniel had never
seen before. "There's nothing spoiled here, ma'am,"
Hannah said. "Maybe it's coming from outside."

"It hardly seems likely." Mrs. West swept toward the
front door with Daniel behind her. As soon as she
opened the door, she made the kind of noise a person
makes when he's been stuck with a pin. A small pile
of garbage was lying on the doorstep with a rotten egg
on top. It didn't look as if it had been carelessly
dumped from a bucket; it looked as if it had been
arranged.

Mrs. West backed away. "So this is Salem." She put
her handkerchief up to her nose and she talked
through it.

"It's not Salem," Daniel snapped. "It's the Liberty
Boys." He went to the kitchen for the hearth shovel.
"Boston has plenty of liberty activity too. It's what
got us into trouble."

The sight of the garbage seemed to have lengthened
Mrs. West's neck. "The rabble in Boston is often
violent." She brushed against Daniel as she hurried
toward the kitchen. "But this is *crudity*! Crudity!"
She swung around and faced Daniel as if he had been
the one to put the garbage there. "Back country
crudity! Why should they pick on the doctor?"

It was a question Daniel couldn't answer. He supposed the Liberty Boys were simply warming up for the
review today. He took the garbage out to the backyard
and buried it. Then he washed down the step. By the
time he returned to the kitchen, *she* had finished her
breakfast and gone upstairs. The whole episode had

upset her stomach, Dr. West explained, and she was lying down for a while before getting ready for the wagonload of her possessions due to arrive later in the morning.

As soon as he'd eaten, Daniel went to the silver drawer for the letter to the governor. He and Beckett would want to get the signatures before noon, when the governor and his party were due to parade with the regiment from Danvers Plain to the Common. Later in the afternoon they could leave the letter at Colonel Browne's, where the governor was staying.

But when Daniel opened the drawer, the letter wasn't there. He pulled the drawer out as far as he could to make sure the letter hadn't got wedged in the back, but it hadn't.

"Did you take a letter out of here, Hannah?" he asked.

Hannah said she hadn't taken it out. She had seen a paper of some sort when she'd set the table at noon the day before but she hadn't touched it. Neither had Dr. West, neither had Sarah.

She must have taken the letter, Daniel thought angrily and he slammed the drawer shut. *She* wouldn't have found a piece of paper in a silver drawer to her liking and, of course, she'd throw it out. He stalked toward the back door, but Dr. West called him back.

"You'll be needed here this morning, Daniel," he said. "We have a lot of work to do. As soon as your mother comes down, we'll be moving furniture out to the barn to make room for her belongings. The wagon should be arriving by midmorning."

Daniel stood in the doorway, his back to the sunlight. "Today is the review," he said.

"I know. I know. The timing is unfortunate."

Unfortunate! "Aren't you going to the review?"

Dr. West was leaning over the fire, rearranging a log, pushing it back a few inches, poking the embers underneath. "Your mother and I will present our compliments at Colonel Browne's later in the afternoon."

"But our letter to the governor!" Daniel insisted. It wasn't as if his father hadn't known about the letter or as if there wasn't time to write another letter quickly and still get signatures.

"Yes, it's a pity." Dr. West's back was bent over the hearth.

A pity! His father had brought home a strange woman; he was disrupting one of the best days of the year and all he could pinch out was a word like *pity*.

"If the wagon arrives in time," Dr. West said, "we may be through before the review is over."

Daniel stood with his hand on the door, jiggling the latch up and down. "Well," he said at last, "I'll have to tell Beckett. I'll be back in a few minutes."

Daniel had seen Beckett the evening before, so at least he didn't have to tell him about *her*. They stood by the pump in the Foote's backyard, each one studying his own shoes, talking in chopped-up sentences. Daniel suggested that Beckett write a letter. He could carry on by himself but Beckett said no, forget it. Then Beckett offered to help with the furniture but Daniel said no, forget it. No point in both of them missing out. Besides, he said, it depended on what time the wagon arrived.

By the time Daniel got back, *she* was downstairs, fully recovered, going from room to room, pointing out the things that were to be taken to the barn. His mother's blue love seat. The candle table with the burn on top. The mirror over the mantelpiece that held the reflection of the conch shell before it. The rocker with the cushion his mother had embroidered the year Sarah was born. At first it was all Daniel could do to hold his tongue as one by one she discarded the things his mother had valued, but then as he got into the work, lifting and carrying and walking, he decided it was best this way. At least he wouldn't be forever plagued by the sight of *her* using his mother's things. The physical labor was something of a release too, as if his body was accomplishing what his mind refused to do. By noon the major part of the past would be covered and stored away, he thought. Under a separate roof. As for the present, he wasn't thinking beyond the arrival of the wagon; he wasn't wishing for anything except that it would come.

Daniel and his father worked without talking. Each one carried an end of the love seat, walking sideways, not even acknowledging the horse who looked curiously over the top of his stall as they passed. His father had swept out a corner of the barn and placed everything meticulously to take up the least room. The four-poster bed had been taken apart and leaned against the wall. The rocker had been upended, a barrel of china had been rolled under the candle table. Over the whole thing they draped old cloths and newspapers.

By eleven o'clock the work was done and still the wagon hadn't arrived. Daniel paced the bare-looking parlor, his eye on the clock, one of the few things that had been allowed to remain in the room. It was a mantel clock with a painted country scene just below its face—a small white farmhouse, two poplar trees, a winding brook, and a little girl in a pink dress, waving. No matter how many times the minute hand jerked from point to point around its circular path, that little girl never lowered her arm, those trees never dropped their leaves. They were shut up in a box with time itself and they didn't move. Daniel went over to the clock and glared at the little girl. "If you were real," he said, "you'd move all right. That minute hand would push you this way and that and there'd be nothing you could do about it."

At twenty minutes past eleven Sarah ran in from the corner with the news that the wagon was in sight. Another ten minutes and it was finally at the house and they were all there to meet it.

The driver, a short, plump man with his face full of tobacco, climbed slowly down from his seat. He assembled his tobacco on one side of his mouth and grinned out of the other. "Been a little later," he said, "I would have led the parade into town." He went to the back of the wagon and let down the tailgate.

Daniel was already up on a wheel, untying the rope that held things together. It was an enormous load.

101

It would take two people over an hour just to get it in the house.

"You see any signs of the parade?" he asked.

"Didn't see anything. Heard the fifes warming up. Over Danvers way."

Mrs. West was standing at the end of the wagon looking over the contents to make sure nothing had been harmed during the trip. "If you go in the back door," she said to the driver, "you'll find the cook has your noon meal laid aside."

The driver grinned and as he loped off toward the kitchen, Daniel and his father began unloading.

Daniel didn't pay any attention to what he was unloading; he just climbed into the wagon, handling barrels and trunks and pieces of furniture as though they were nameless objects, each one simply an impediment to his freedom. The smaller things were in the house when he heard the fifes faintly in the distance, then louder, whistling up the people of Salem. Doors were flung open and folks ran laughing to King Street to follow the parade. Daniel was standing in the wagon, holding one end of the sofa as the tinman ran past, untying his leather apron as he went. Sarah joined the family of a neighbor and she went too.

Dr. West lifted his end of the sofa as though he hadn't heard a thing. The music passed, the sound of marching feet passed, the huzzaing cries of the onlookers retreated—all toward the Common. The bed came next—six separate trips, for the bottom, the mattress, the four sides. It was an awkward thing to move because of the long posts on which the canopy would be fitted. It was on the second trip into the house that Dr. West stopped in the kitchen. The driver was still at the table, lingering over a piece of mince pie.

Dr. West leaned against the doorway. "I suppose for a price," he said, "you might be willing to help me finish unloading and set up the furniture in the house."

The driver grinned. "For a price and another piece of mince pie," he said, "I'd be willing to do anything."

Dr. West nodded at Daniel. He didn't need to say more and Daniel didn't take time for anything but a quick thanks. He streaked to the front door.

"You folks eat when you've a mind to," he called over his shoulder. "I'll get something from Hannah when I get back." Then as an afterthought he added, "Or someplace."

The regiment was in formation when Daniel finally arrived, panting, at the outskirts of the crowd. Beckett had stationed himself on top of a wide rock on the edge of the Common so Daniel would be sure to spot him.

"Got us a good viewing position, I see," Daniel grinned, jumping up beside Beckett. He felt as if he'd been holding his breath all morning and slowly he let it out as Beckett pointed out the men on horseback— the governor with his back to the boys, General Brattle, Mr. Richard Saltonstall, high sheriff of Essex County, and over to one side near Colonel Browne, commander of the regiment, was a pleasant mild-faced man who sat his horse smartly enough but looked less military than the others.

"Secretary Flucker," Beckett said. He was the man

whose signature appeared at the bottom of all the governor's orders. Daniel had often wondered about him, thinking it would be nice to sign one's name on documents that would be preserved through history. Daniel observed the neat way Secretary Flucker's hair was rolled into three rows of curls over his ears; he noted the precise way he held the reins of his horse. Yes, Daniel decided, Secretary Flucker likely wrote a good *y* and took pains with his capital *F*.

Then suddenly the review began. The adjutant called out the first order.

"Beat the long roll!" he called in a thunderous voice. The drummers, standing with the fifers on the west side of the field, went into action. Hard and fast the drums rattled, each beat distinct from the one before, followed immediately by the next one, never pausing for a breath, until the hard, hollow tattoo beat seemed to have set the whole day throbbing. Daniel wondered that the regiment could stand so still, but then as quickly as the drumming had begun, it was over and the call came for the trooping of the colors. The Great Union and the regimental flag were passed down the ranks and the fifes had their turn, running up and down the scale while the drums beat an undercurrent.

As grand as the review was to watch, Daniel decided, it was grander to hear—the muskets all clicking at the same time as they were shouldered or put at rest, the orders all ending with a bark, like a word kicked into the field, and the music whistling and beating its way under a person's skin so that he wanted to stand up and tell the king he was ready, ready for anything.

Daniel glanced at Jeremy, whom he had spotted in the crowd, standing with a group of Whig friends. Surely, Daniel thought, Jeremy couldn't help but know, listening to the music, that the king was their friend and that the British Empire was meant to last forever.

The music stopped and Daniel held his breath while, one after another, the orders for firing muskets were called.

"Advance Firelocks!"

"Handle Cartridge!"

"Bite Cartridge!" Daniel imagined he could feel the end of a cartridge between his own teeth as each infantryman bit off the paper that exposed the powder.

"Prime Pan!"

"Shut Pan!"

"Cast About!" The guns were dropped to the ground, butt down, locks up to hold the powder in place.

"Charge Firelock!"

"Draw Rammer!" The soldiers drew out their rammers and inserted them into the tips of the barrels.

"Ram!"

"Return Rammer!"

"Poise Firelock!" Up and down the lines muskets were brought at full cock to shoulders while men held their faces back from the firelocks. Along with the soldiers, Daniel's head reared back and his eyes squinted.

"GIVE FIRE!"

There it was, the final blazing, thundering outburst,

the end to the suspense, the glorious culmination to everything. Then again it built up and again the world exploded. Again and again. The fife and drum corps played "God Save the King" and when the regiment finally marched off the field, the drums accompanied them with "The British Grenadiers."

Every muscle in Daniel's body had been tensed throughout the review and now he felt as if he'd been dropped limp onto the Common.

"How did it make you feel?" Beckett asked.

"Loyal," Daniel said. "Loyal."

Beckett nodded. "I know."

"Wonder how Charlie and Benjie felt."

"Haven't seen them."

When they thought about it, they realized they hadn't seen any of the Whig boys, nor for that matter many of the most outspoken adults, which probably explained the fact that the review had passed without incident or rudeness. But to make sure they hadn't overlooked any Whig friends, Beckett and Daniel began walking around the Common.

"Charlie and Benjie couldn't be *that* high for liberty that they'd miss this," Daniel insisted.

Beckett shook his head. "Daft. That's what they are."

The only person they saw from school was Peter Ray and he was standing under the chestnut tree with Sam White and Edward Pine, the two apprentices who had so provoked Daniel the day that Ding-Dong Allison had held forth.

"Nice company Peter's keeping," Beckett observed.

Daniel grinned. "As long as he's off my neck." It

was the one good thing *she* had accomplished, he thought.

The crowd had mostly dispersed now and the Common was taken over by children. Scraggly groups of boys equipped themselves with sticks and barked orders at each other. One small towhead, beside himself with excitement, ran around in circles, going off like a gun. Two bigger boys, ten- or eleven-year-olds, went careening across the field with hoops and hoopsticks, playing the post office game all young Salem boys played in the spring. They looked behind to make sure no one was following them, then raced after their hoops—on their way, Daniel supposed, to their secret hiding place.

Daniel and Beckett had dropped down on the grass, loath to leave the Common.

"Remember our hoop days?" Daniel asked.

"We had the best hiding places."

At the beginning of every spring Salem boys paired off and established hiding places or post offices where they deposited the tiny newspapers they made and attached as invisibly as possible to their hoops. It was against the rules to stop another hoop while it was rolling. The point of the game was to establish as many post offices as you could and try to find other people's post offices. When you did, you were entitled to take the newspaper that was hidden there and hide it in your own home office, which, of course, was the most secret place of all. Then on the first of June the couple who could exhibit the most stolen newspapers were the winners, the Grand Postmasters of the year.

"No one ever did find our home office," Beckett said. "You remember where it was?"

"Of course."

It had been a long time since Daniel had thought of that oak tree over by Cheevers Pond, not far from the place where the cat had been hanged the night of Judge Ropes' death. There was a large knothole in the tree above the reaching height of young boys; either Daniel or Beckett had to stand on the other's back in order to get to it. They had kept the entrance to the hole filled with dead leaves so that a person passing, happening to glance that way, would have no suspicions.

"Wonder if anyone has used it since," Daniel said.

Without a word the two boys got up and walked toward Cheevers Pond. The tree didn't seem as tall as it had once; the knothole was easily within reach and there were no leaves blocking the entrance.

"Likely a squirrel has taken over," Beckett said, reaching up.

"Well, watch out you don't get bitten."

From the expression on Beckett's face as he put his hand in the hole, Daniel judged that Beckett had struck something that surprised him. When he brought his hand out, he was holding a piece of paper. It was a fairly small piece of paper but only a single sheet, roughly torn, not like the long, thin folded sheets they had used to fit to the inside of their hoops. Nor was it made in any way to simulate a newspaper. There were only three words on the paper. HOLD YOUR FIRE! it said.

"The boys today must be playing the game differently," Beckett said.

"Lazy playing," Daniel agreed, remembering how they had struggled over the tiny letters, working them into the language of the *Essex Gazette*.

"Looks like fresh writing."

"Well, let's put it back. We don't want to interfere with the work of the Grand Postmasters of the year."

But it was a strange message, Daniel thought. And likely because the firing orders were so fresh in his mind, he had a queer feeling. As if somewhere a gun was being held in a half-cocked position and the priming and the ramming were still to come.

Chapter Seven

T ILLIE HAD BEEN entertaining queer feelings, too. Jeremy said it was only because she was unhappy about giving up Jonathon and unhappiness sharpened a person's superstitions. There seemed to be some truth to what Jeremy said because the morning that Jonathon was to leave, Tillie's fears were the most acute.

Daniel had been given permission to stay home from school for the day and take the chaise over to Jeremy's and pick up Tillie and Jonathon.

Tillie, dressed in her Sunday best, was slowly folding the last of Jonathon's clothes and putting them into a case. Her face had a stretched look as though it was all her skin could do to cover the bones.

"I don't know what made me step out of the house last night," she said. "I knew better."

"Now, Til," Jeremy said. "Stop that fretting."

But Tillie wouldn't stop. She turned to Daniel. "I just didn't think. I went out of the house and before I knew it, I looked up and I saw the new moon through the trees."

Daniel knew that the way Tillie looked at it, nothing could be worse luck. More than once on the night of a new moon, he had, with his own eyes lowered, led Tillie blindfolded to a clearing and then, when he thought the view was free from trees, they had both looked up. That way, Tillie said, life was safer for the next month.

"It's just old woman's talk," Jeremy said impatiently, picking up the case to carry it to the chaise. "You're just unhappy to part with Jonathon."

"Of course I'm unhappy," Tillie snapped. "But you know as well as I do that seeing a new moon that way *signifies*. A whole string of bad events in the offing." She stooped down to pick up Jonathon. "Misfortune never travels alone."

Daniel cast about in his mind. It was true; he

couldn't think of a single misfortune that hadn't been
followed by others.

"Unhappiness ahead," Tillie said. "That's what the
new moon was saying all leafed over. You'll see."

Jeremy didn't argue further. He picked up the
cradle and put it in the chaise and then they all climbed
into the seat—Tillie, her lips set, sitting like a rock,
holding Jonathon.

Tillie had already met the new Mrs. West when
she had come with the doctor the week before to see
Jonathon, to make final arrangements, and settle the
financial agreement about Jonathon's care. Tillie had
complained later how she had hated to take money
for something that had given her such joy but once
she'd seen Mrs. West entering the house, holding up
her skirts as if she weren't used to stepping on such
humble ground, she'd known there would be nothing
but business between them. There'd be no talking
about the best way to care for Jonathon, no invitations
to see how Jonathon was progressing, no future at all.

On the way to the West house, Tillie's face grew
tauter and tighter and when they were finally inside
and she handed the baby over to Mrs. West, Tillie
was like a block of granite and Jonathon, for all anyone could tell, might have been a sack of potatoes
she'd stored over the winter.

Daniel couldn't bear to think of Jeremy and Tillie
going back to that empty house, so when Jonathon was
settled, he suggested that the three of them take a walk
around town. Jeremy quickly agreed. It had been a

long time, he said, since Tillie had been free to take a walk. She hadn't seen the violets in the Common; she hadn't been to the harbor in five months.

Tillie was like Jeremy about the sea; it gave her release to look at it, and now on Derby Wharf, the wind whipping her skirts, she sighed. It was as if she were saying, "Well, at least the sea is still here." In the outgoing tide all the boats were pointed toward Marblehead, their masts rising and falling with the water. One by one, Jeremy named the ships, calling them out loudly over the noise of the wind and the waves.

Behind Derby Wharf the bell from East Church began to ring but the sound of the sea was strong and no one paid any attention. Then the bell from the East Church was joined by bells from other churches. Louder and more urgent they became until not even the wind and the waves could deny them.

The three people on the wharf turned around.

"The bells aren't pealing," Jeremy said. "They're tolling."

Tillie gathered up her skirts and began walking fast down the wharf. "I told you," she said. "I told you."

On the waterfront people were running toward King Street. Mr. Palfrey, the sailmaker, ran past the other way. "It's the News!" he cried. "It's come! Posted up at the Town House. They're closing Boston Harbor!"

There was a large crowd around the Town House, but they weren't talking. People at the front of the crowd read the notice that was nailed there and then

113

they moved away to make room for others as if everyone sensed a person's need to read the words for himself.

When Jeremy and Tillie and Daniel finally reached the front, they saw two papers nailed to the board beside the Town House door. Both were titled *The Boston Port Bill*; one was in official language and the other was signed by the Committee of Correspondence with a skull and crossbones at the top and bordered with a wide band of black mourning.

Daniel read the official one first. *WHEREAS*, it began in large capital letters. It went on in smaller print; then came more capital letters: *BE IT ENACTED*. This was followed by a string of *noes*. "*No* vessel, lighter, boat, or bottom, *no* goods, wares or merchandise whatever . . . *no* . . . *no*."

The Committee of Correspondence had put the bill into simpler language. "They have ordered our port to be entirely shut up, leaving us barely so much of the means of subsistence as to keep us from perishing from cold and hunger. A fleet of British war ships is to block our harbor . . . until obedience is paid to the laws and authority of Great Britain."

When Daniel had finished reading, he looked at Jeremy and saw that they were both thinking the same thoughts. The king had not understood. Every word in the Boston Port Bill was harsh and unbending, not even admitting that although the Tea Party might have been ill-advised, there was cause for discontent and need for discussion. As for the Punishment, anyone who lived in a harbor town knew that the Punishment could scarcely have been more severe. In Boston, as in Salem, the whole means of living was tied up in the harbor. The king meant to starve Boston into submission, as if America were a schoolroom and he could establish order by reducing the most lively student to groveling humility. And there was more punishment, apparently, yet to come. Further acts relating to Massachusetts, it was announced, would be arriving soon.

"He didn't leave us a single loophole," Jeremy said as they gave up their places in front of the Town House. "No way we could go through the motions of amends if we'd a mind to, with honor." He linked his arm with Tillie's. "You were right this time, Til," he said. "All we can do is to unite behind Boston. And hope that at least the new governor, whoever he is, will be more understanding."

Suddenly Daniel didn't want to hear any more Whig talk. He didn't like thinking about the king as he'd been thinking. He'd let his thoughts run away with him. Now he wanted to be with Tory people and hear Tory talk about the Port Bill.

"It's about dinnertime," he said. "I guess I'll go home."

Daniel had supposed the gloom from the town would have spread into his own house, but no one seemed overly concerned. Hannah was just taking a fried chicken from the fireplace as Daniel arrived. The doctor and Sarah were already at the table and Mrs. West was coming downstairs from attending Jonathon. It was a normal meal as if the bells hadn't been tolling all morning.

"You heard, didn't you?" Daniel asked, slipping into his place at the table.

Dr. West nodded, then bowed his head and thanked the Lord for all His blessings. When he looked up, he summed up the Port Bill in three words: "Our just deserts."

Daniel began cutting the meat from a chicken leg. "Only a few people had a hand in the Tea Party," he said, "but everyone will have to suffer. It doesn't seem fair."

"Suffer?" Dr. West shrugged. "All Boston has to do is pay for the tea. All she has to do is show she's ready to acknowledge Britain's authority."

"Jeremy says Boston can't pay with honor. Not without sacrificing the right of people to govern themselves."

Mrs. West put her fork down sharply on her plate. "People who approve of throwing away a cargo of tea are hardly in a position to prate about honor. Honor," she said, "is a gentleman's word."

Daniel knotted his hands under the table, sorry that he'd brought up the subject at all.

As soon as dinner was over, he went upstairs, paid Jonathon a visit, then he left to find Beckett. Instead of turning to the right at the corner to go to Beckett's, however, he turned left, noticing a group of people in front of Goodhue's Tavern. Beckett was at the edge of the group. He pointed at a stranger who seemed to be the center of attention.

"The Committee member from Boston," Beckett explained. "The one who brought the notice. He's just taken dinner at Goodhue's." He nodded toward the tavern hitching post. "Look who's been taking care of his horse."

Benjie and Charlie were holding up a pail of water for the Committee member's horse.

"Wonder if they got the news first," Daniel said. "They were so all-fired anxious."

Beckett shrugged. "Makes no difference. No chance of their making up with us now."

They headed for the Common, walking quickly past the flag, which had been dropped to half-mast. The morning wind had died and the flag drooped by the pole, the red cross of St. George lost in the folds.

"Let's go where there's nothing to remind us," Beckett said, and so it was that they found themselves near Cheevers Pond, going past the oak tree they had visited two weeks before.

Daniel put his hand into the knothole. "Let's see how our post office successors are making out."

He drew out a piece of paper rough torn like the last one. The message was even stranger. At the top was the date, May 11. It had been written that very day. Under this was a short column of words that didn't at first glance make much sense.

Give fire
Allison
Midnight

"Funniest newspaper I've ever seen," Beckett remarked but then, as they puzzled over it, they both
grinned. The kids in town were after old Ding-Dong
Allison again, going to smoke him out most likely, and
the time was midnight—pretty late for post-office-aged
boys—but Beckett and Daniel had crept out of their
own homes at that age often enough to know it was
possible with careful planning to muster quite a group
for midnight fun.

Daniel put the note back, feeling envious of the
ten- and eleven-year-olds who on a day like today with
the rest of Salem submerged in gloom had nothing on
their minds but schoolboy pranks.

"Let's go watch them," Daniel said. "We'll get there
early and find a hiding place."

Just as in the old days, they began making plans,
where they would meet, how they would get out of
their houses without arousing their parents' suspicions.

At eleven o'clock Daniel and Beckett met at the
corner of King Street.

"Libera!" Daniel grinned.

"Libera," Beckett replied.

When they'd been younger, they had, as all boys did,
pretended to be Indians on a stolen night out, creeping
through the shadows, hiding behind trees. Daniel often
thought that it must have been such boyhood games

118

that had inspired the men in Boston to dress like Mohawks for the Tea Party and although, as a Tory, Daniel had disapproved of the Tea Party, he had, in spite of himself, admired the way it had been carried out—grown men in masquerade reviving their youth without a single misstep. So Daniel and Beckett slipped silently among the trees of the Common, and the not quite new moon, like a smile in the sky, shone down on them.

Mr. Allison's shack was not far from the Almshouse on the river end of the Common. All but hidden among the pine trees, it was a tumbledown affair made of odd-shaped boards pieced together. Looking at it, Daniel and Beckett agreed it was an ideal place for a smoking. The roof would be easily reached by climbing on Mr. Allison's pigpen, which leaned against the house. Then all a person had to do was to cover the top of the chimney so the smoke would back up in the house. There was only one door to be blocked and one window, a pine slab of a shutter over a hole in the wall, already closed. Daniel figured that six young boys could do the job—two on the roof, two each to brace the door and window so old Ding-Dong couldn't get out until he'd cried all the *pretty pleases* and *kiss your shoes* that the boys required of him.

Daniel and Beckett found a concealed spot on the pigpen side of the house where they could see both the roof and the front door. They lay down on their stomachs, nudging each other and pointing to the plume of smoke that rose from the chimney. They had

119

never considered the place at such close quarters or at such length. Nor, indeed, had they smelled it. Both boys pinched their noses.

"I've smelled pigpens before," Beckett whispered, "but this one—whew!"

"Don't see how the pig stands it."

"Maybe there isn't a pig. Didn't see one."

"Maybe it's Ding-Dong we're smelling."

Laughing, the boys were burying their noses in pine needles, trying to replace one smell with another, when they heard footsteps approaching from the Common.

Daniel expected at any moment that the single footsteps would merge into a running scuffle as the boys came, giggling together before the shack.

Then out of the shadows the first figure appeared. It was not a boy, or if it was, it was certainly one who had left his hoop-rolling days far behind. It was a tall figure, followed by two others whose faces in the dark were undistinguishable. They waited a moment, then were joined by three more. Each of them carried a bucket. The group walked up the steps to the shack, knocked, then stood at the doorway as the door was opened and the light from the room fell upon them.

There was no doubt now who they were. Three of them were strangers to Beckett and Daniel. They were tall, slouching young men wearing fisherman hats, the kind that were worn by Marbleheaders. But they weren't the ones that Daniel and Beckett were staring at. Behind them were Sam White and Edward Pine and at the foot of the steps, standing by himself but obviously one of the group, was Peter Ray.

Ding-Dong Allison was framed in the doorway, his long gray hair straggling at his shoulders.

"Small group tonight, eh?"

There was no answer.

"Well, it don't matter. All we got now is small jobs."

Edward Pine shuffled his feet. "We're ready for a bigger job, Mr. Allison."

"Bigger ones are comin'. When the time is ripe. And who says when the time is ripe?"

"You do, Mr. Allison." Edward Pine mumbled his reply.

"All right. All we want to do now is to get under the Tories' skin. We overstep ourselves and we'll be put out of business. You all got your buckets?" Ding-Dong looked around the group, nodded, and then he pointed his finger at Peter Ray.

"There's our convert," he said. "Seen the light, have you?"

Peter was struggling with a fresh cold. He took a deep sniff. "Yes, sir," he said.

"You know I don't take to young folks and young folks don't take to me. You know that, do you?"

"Yes, sir."

"It's only the needs of the times that's got us working together. I see the needs and you do the work. You understand?"

"Yes, sir."

"That way, your natural orneriness will be put to a constructive end. And all you boys, you know the end."

"Yes, sir." The answer came in a chorus.

"Let's hear it."

"Damnation to Tories!"

Ding-Dong stepped aside and all six boys, including Peter Ray, set their buckets on the porch and walked into the house. The door closed and in a moment the plume of smoke thickened at the chimney as though a fresh log might have been thrown on the fire.

"Whew!" It was Beckett who made the noise as if all the air had been pumped out of him. There was no need to discuss what they'd seen. It was obvious that these were the Liberty Boys, at least some of them, and that Ding-Dong Allison was their leader. It was also obvious that Peter Ray had turned traitor. As for the buckets, there was no mystery about them. The pigpen smell was nothing compared to the smell from the front porch. Unquestionably, the buckets contained the evening's supply of Liberty Gifts.

The two boys lay on the pine needles, letting the knowledge of what they had seen slowly soak into them. The house was like a box with only a crack of light showing around the edges of the door and no way either to peek in to see what was taking place or to listen to what was being said.

"We must never let on that we know," Beckett said at last, but Daniel's thoughts had been traveling another course. He had a pine cone in his hand and he was breaking it into shreds.

"We've got to get Peter Ray," he said. "We've got to get him good."

"No!" Beckett whispered the word and Daniel was

surprised at the urgency he gave it. "No!" he repeated. "We must keep this secret and not even let Peter suspect. We've got a source of useful information in that old oak tree. No telling how useful."

Daniel shifted his thinking and was trying to send his mind after Beckett's when Ding-Dong Allison's door opened again.

The six boys came out and picked up their buckets. Ding-Dong stood in the doorway.

"Cobweb britches to all Tories," he said.

"And a hedgehog saddle," the boys replied.

"A hard trotting horse," Ding-Dong said.

"And constant riding."

The boys raised their buckets. "Down with King George!"

Ding-Dong closed his door and the six boys disappeared through the pine trees. As soon as it was safe, Beckett and Daniel got up.

"Let's follow them," Beckett whispered.

Keeping at a distance but within sound of the footsteps, the two boys crept through the woods, pausing at the edge of the Common to see which direction the Liberty Boys were taking, then silently skirting the fields into town.

Once they were among houses, it was easier. Crouching behind walls, lying flat beside fences, they kept the Liberty Boys in sight, sometimes from more than a block away. They were not surprised that the first stop was Colonel Browne's. One of the boys crept up to the door while the rest waited. He emptied his bucket, returned to the boys, spoke, and then slunk away by himself while the other five went on. One by one, as they deposited their gifts, they dropped off and the rest proceeded, their company diminishing as they went.

Somewhere, however, Daniel and Beckett lost the group. They didn't see them again until they were on the river end of Daniel's street and then they caught sight of two boys approaching Colonel Frye's house. One of the boys left his gift, then he, too, walked away.

The last boy went on alone. By going through backyards, Daniel and Beckett decided they could get ahead of the boy and still not be seen. They'd get under cover of the honeysuckle that grew beside Daniel's house and watch which way the boy turned at the corner.

They were barely established when they heard a series of sniffs coming up the road. Beckett poked Daniel. The last boy was Peter Ray.

He didn't go to the corner. He turned in at Daniel's house and walked up the steps. Daniel and Beckett peeked through the honeysuckle over the floor of the porch. Peter Ray turned the bucket upside down, reached into his coat pocket, took out an egg, broke it on top of the pile, spat, and walked off.

When Peter left, Daniel was ready to run after him but Beckett put his hand over Daniel's mouth and his knee into Daniel's stomach.

"You're going to spoil everything, Daniel West," he hissed. "Are you more interested in Peter Ray or are you more interested in the Tory cause?"

Gradually Daniel let his anger subside. "The Tory cause," he said and Beckett let him go.

The two of them cleaned up the mess on Daniel's doorstep and said good night.

Chapter Eight

TILLIE KNITTED her way through the month of May.
She rocked before the fireplace, clicking her
needles as if she could rock and click away not only
her private heartache over the loss of Jonathon but
the public heartache over the condition of Massachusetts. Every row of stitches represented a block of time

126

she had somehow managed to get through in that quiet house where the only news that came was bad news.

She barely looked up the day that Jeremy came in and said that the new governor of Massachusetts had arrived in Boston. "General Thomas Gage," he said. "Commander of British forces in America."

Tillie nodded. "A military man."

"Well, he knows the country. He's spent eighteen years here."

"Governor Hutchison knew the country too," Tillie pointed out.

"Maybe General Gage is different. He's married to an American wife."

"Wives!" Tillie scoffed. "What good are wives?"

Jeremy smiled and dropped his hand on Tillie's shoulder. "We couldn't get along without them," he said.

But there came a day when Jeremy had news so extraordinary that Tillie forgot all about her knitting. Daniel was sitting on a footstool, holding a skein of wool in both hands and Tillie was winding it into a ball when Jeremy came into the room. He put his hat down on the table.

"Boston," he said, "is no longer the capital of Massachusetts. We have a new capital."

It was like saying that London had been moved up the Thames River. It was a geographic fact and Daniel had never known a geographic fact to be changed—poof!—like that.

"What's the new capital?"

Jeremy looked as though he couldn't make up his mind if he liked the idea or not.

"Salem," he said.

"Salem!" Daniel and Tillie repeated the word together. Tillie stood up. Her knitting dropped to the floor.

"For the time being anyway," Jeremy said. "The General Court will meet here the first week in June. The new governor thinks that Salem will be more friendly than Boston."

Tillie sat down, her hands idle in her lap. "He better have another think," she said.

Daniel had to get used to the news. On the way home, he looked at Salem, trying to see it as the seat of government, the place that would take up the argument with the king. There was the Town House, for instance, where the General Court would convene. And Mr. Goodhue's Tavern. In a few weeks, it would house the most important men in the province—Mr. Paine, Mr. Cushing, Mr. Daniel Leonard, the prominent Tory. These men would be walking the narrow streets that Daniel was walking and while they did, they'd be making history, one way or another.

And Mr. Samuel Adams. He'd be here too. Daniel sighed. Samuel Adams was the man folks said was behind all the trouble, a rabble-rouser who'd planned the Tea Party. He'd be right here in Salem. He was one person Daniel thought he'd recognize. He'd have to be a wild-eyed, quick-talking man, always in a hurry, Daniel figured, never looking where he was going.

If Daniel had to weigh the news before deciding if he liked it, Hannah didn't. It was clear when Daniel walked into the house that she didn't like it at all. She was banging pots and pans around the kitchen.

"It's too much," she muttered. "On top of everything else!"

Daniel didn't see how the news could make so much difference to Hannah. "What's wrong with it?" he asked.

"What's wrong?" Hannah cried. She grabbed a dish towel from its nail on the wall. "Mr. Daniel Leonard is going to be staying here," she said. "That's what's wrong. He's a friend of *hers*." She jerked her head in the direction of the upper floor and then she flapped her dish towel. "Right here in this house. The Tory leader. Eating and sleeping."

"Here?" Daniel sat down on the stool.

"That's what I said. Here. And he's so important, the whole house has to be turned inside out for his coming. Cooking and cleaning, cleaning and cooking, I'll be on the run for a month."

She was already on the run, Daniel noted, thinking what a strange thing it was that history and geography could reach right into a person's kitchen.

Within a few days all of Salem was fitting itself out for the General Court. Carpenters were at the Town House, rushing to make new seats to accommodate the many representatives. Even those who were not directly concerned with feeding or housing the Court were caught up in the contagion of work. Shutters on private homes that had been banging for months were made fast; shaky steps were mended; clean curtains were hung at windows; signs that had faded were given a fresh coat of paint. Seamstresses and milliners worked around the clock to fill the orders of the ladies of Salem.

On June first the Port of Boston was officially closed. Out of sympathy, all the Whig churches muffled their clappers and tolled. But if that day called for grief, the next day, as it turned out, called for despair.

On June second the further Acts of Parliament, which had been promised, arrived. They were more severe than even the most pessimistic people had predicted.

The Committee of Correspondence had labeled the first act "The Murder Bill." It said that disturbers of the King's peace would be transported out of the province for trial—either to England or a place designated by the governor.

The second act said that the members of the Council were not to be elected by the people any more; they were to be appointed by the Crown. And after August first there were to be no more town meetings without the written consent of the governor.

No more town meetings! Daniel and Sarah were on their way into town to do an errand for Mrs. West when they read the notice posted on the Town House.

"What does it mean?" Sarah whispered.

Daniel set his mouth in a grim line. "It means," he said, "that we can't decide anything. It will all be the governor's doing."

Daniel hardly expected Sarah to understand. Still,

even an eight-year-old ought to know better than to smile. "Why, it will be easier this way," she said. "One man deciding. Mother says now every Tom, Dick, and Harry thinks he can run the government."

Daniel flushed. "Easier?" he said. "It takes the pride right out of being a man."

Sarah thought about that a moment then she came up with her second question. "Why do they call it the Murder Bill?"

"If the governor wants to, he can arrest Sam Adams and John Hancock right now and send them to England to stand trial."

"Well, everyone says we'd be better off without them."

"Maybe. Maybe." Daniel sighed. "The Whigs wouldn't say so. They'd say Sam Adams wouldn't stand a chance in a place where he didn't have any friends, a place that has set itself up against the colonies."

Sarah tossed her head. "Well, I know what Mother would say. She'd say 'Good riddance,' and I say so too."

"What do you know?" Daniel grabbed Sarah's hand and pulled her along. After all, the English soldiers who had fired at the Boston Massacre had been acquitted in this country. He wasn't ready to believe that the Massachusetts courts were wholly unfair or that the charter could be wiped out with just a snap of the fingers.

"It's up to the new governor," he said more to himself than to Sarah. "He's the one who will carry out the acts. It all depends on what kind of a man he is."

Within a few days Daniel began to get a taste of what it was to live in the capital of a province. Not only did the representatives begin to arrive but strangers came too—peddlers, salesmen, lawyers, scribes, Committee members, curious people from neighboring towns, young folks looking for excitement or perhaps trouble—anyone who for profit or pleasure or political reasons wanted to be near the center of activity. Daniel Leonard was not among the early arrivals, but Sam Adams was. The news was hissed around town but with the Murder Bill out, Daniel figured Mr. Adams wouldn't likely show himself too freely.

Several of the representatives had been pointed out to Daniel, however—Robert Treat Paine and John Bowdoin, both Whigs, and Elisha Jones, a tavern keeper from Weston and a Tory. But the representatives spent most of their time in closed rooms, conferring, and Salem people didn't have much chance to get acquainted. There was only one man that Daniel kept seeing time and again and he obviously wasn't a representative but a hanger-on of some kind. He was a rather slack-faced, self-effacing man who looked as if he slept in his clothes, if he slept at all. He seemed to spend all his time walking with a slow shuffle from one end of Salem to another, stopping to talk with anyone and everyone who had a word to spare. Daniel saw him the first time sitting idly on a keg of molasses down at the dock, talking with a group of sailors. He seemed to be drawn to idle folk, which struck Daniel as somewhat curious because if he had something to sell, he wasn't approaching a likely market.

Another day Daniel saw the stranger in the Common and he was talking to Ding-Dong Allison. Obviously he didn't know much to be wasting his time on Mr. Allison and Daniel had just about decided he must be one of those traveling fortune-tellers or astrologists that he'd heard about, foretelling futures to folks who thought the stars had something to do with the way bread rose or sickness came to your door. So it was a surprise to Daniel when he saw the stranger the next time under such different circumstances and with such different company.

It came about one afternoon when Daniel had decided to go inside the Town House to see the new seats that had been constructed. Before going upstairs to the room where the representatives would meet, he stopped in the downstairs courtroom because it was a place that never failed to give him the shivers. Stepping into that room, Daniel felt, was the closest he could get to England, closer even than when he was on the end of Derby Wharf looking out across the water. High on the northern wall were the royal arms of Great Britain held up by the lion and the unicorn. Looking at it was like listening to the Fife and Drum Corps beat the long roll. Here he was, he told himself—Daniel West, part of the British Empire—and there were the lion and unicorn protecting him as they had protected British subjects for generation after generation.

It was when a person turned around and looked at

the other walls that he realized afresh what a new experiment America was, how close it still was to its raw beginnings. Hanging on the other walls were a number of dried and shriveled Algonquin Indian scalps, relics of the bloody wars of earlier times. Daniel remembered how he and Beckett in their younger days had taken such a morbid interest in the scalps; once they had even dared each other to touch one. Today, however, they made Daniel angry. With all the renovation Salem had done, he thought, it was a wonder they couldn't have taken down those dirty things. He was standing partway behind the half-opened door, looking up at a particularly gruesome specimen with a long black pigtail hanging down the wall, when he heard steps in the corridor outside.

The steps approached but, instead of coming into the room, they went past the door on the way to the stairs at the other end of the hall. Daniel looked through the crack in the door as two men walked by. He recognized one as Robert Treat Paine, the Whig representative from Taunton. The other man was the stranger, the fortune-teller if that's what he was. The two men stopped down the hall and Daniel could hear them clearly.

"Everything quiet?" Mr. Paine asked.

"I've seen to that. There'll be no trouble, I think."

"I've been talking conciliation."

"Yes," the stranger said, "that's the way. Daniel Leonard is the only thorn I can see."

"Well," Mr. Paine said, "if we can get the governor out of the way, I can take care of Leonard."

There was no more talking. Daniel heard the two men climb the stairs and then he left the building.

Jeremy was the one Daniel wanted to ask about the stranger but he didn't get a chance to see Jeremy until the next day, the day before the Court was to convene, the day that Mr. Leonard was due to arrive. Daniel walked down to Jeremy's but as he was approaching the house, who should walk out of the door but the stranger himself. If he was a fortune-teller, Daniel thought, Tillie would certainly be a good subject.

As soon as the stranger was out of the way, Daniel burst into Jeremy's house. "What did that man want?" he asked.

Jeremy was sitting at the table but before he could answer, Tillie had to inquire about Jonathon.

"He's fine," Daniel said. "He's so smart, he'll be walking before you know it."

"Ah." Tillie smiled. She was looking forward to the day when Jonathon could walk and Daniel could bring him for a visit.

Daniel turned back to Jeremy. "That man that was here," he repeated. "What did he want?"

"Why, he heard I was the night watchman," Jeremy said, "and he wondered if I didn't want help on my rounds while Court was in session. He didn't want to see any trouble develop."

"He walks enough. Did he think he could pick up some money doing it?"

Jeremy grinned. "He wasn't offering to stand watch himself. But he has friends who could lend a hand."

Daniel sank down into a chair. "Who is that man, Jeremy?"

"You don't know, boy?"

"Of course I don't know," Daniel snapped, "or I wouldn't be asking."

Slowly Jeremy pushed back his chair. "That man," he said, "is Mr. Samuel Adams."

Samuel Adams! Talking peace! It was like finding an odd-shaped piece to a puzzle that a person never dreamed would fit and yet it did. But there were still pieces missing, and before going home Daniel circled into the Common. He went to the oak tree and put his hand into the hole. There, as he had half expected, was a new note.

Sorry, boys, the note said. *You'll have to hold your fire a while longer. Orders from above. No trouble at all.*

Daniel put the note back, puzzling about it as he walked home. Then he had no opportunity to think further about Samuel Adams.

Benjie and the two Thomases were standing at the corner of his street. As Daniel approached, they started to laugh. Thomas Cook began walking with fancy, mincing steps and he swept his hat off his head with a wide, exaggerated gesture. "Your company has arrived, Lord West," he said.

All the boys swept off their hats and bowed. "Mr. Lacey Pants is here," Benjie cackled.

"We didn't know you lived in Windsor Castle, m'lord," Thomas Cook echoed.

"With a chariot and pair," Thomas Clark added, beside himself with glee.

"Oo-la-la!" All the boys took up the chant.

Daniel looked toward his house. In front of it was a chariot, the first chariot that had ever been seen in Salem. Before the chariot was not one horse, but two.

Daniel dropped his eyes, pushed his hands into his pockets, and walked home.

Chapter Nine

D ANIEL SLIPPED into the kitchen, where Hannah was surrounded by cakes, breads, pies, and cookies, some ready to serve, some half prepared. She threw up floured hands when she saw Daniel, jerked her head toward the front room, and rolled her eyes to the ceiling.

"What's he like?" Daniel whispered.

"Fancy," Hannah hissed, putting her hands into a lump of dough. "Highfalutin!"

Daniel picked up a cookie, stopping at the cradle, which was in the kitchen today. Jonathon was lying on his back, playing with his teething ring.

"Go in and see for yourself," Hannah said.

Daniel ate the cookie, then walked into the front room. As he entered, the conversation stopped abruptly.

"So this is the young man we were speaking of," Mr. Leonard said, rising and flicking a speck of dust from his coat sleeve. Daniel hardly had a chance to wonder at this statement; he was too busy taking in Mr. Leonard. He could see why Benjie had called him Mr. Lacey Pants. He was covered with lace—narrow lace on his shirt, gold lace on his coat and a broader band of gold lace on the hat that lay on the table beside him. He was friendly enough and likable in a way, but when Daniel studied his features, he decided that Mr. Leonard was as hard and stubborn as a rock. He looked, in fact, like a refined bulldog.

The thing that troubled Daniel most was the voices; all that laciness had affected everyone's voice. Mrs. West's voice had climbed an octave since Mr. Leonard's arrival and Sarah, in imitation, had sent hers so high, it seemed to be coming out of her eyes. As for Dr. West, he was searching for peace in the lower registers.

Daniel listened to his own voice as he answered Mr. Leonard's questions about his schooling. "No," he said, "Mr. Nicholls is not a good teacher. I haven't made up my mind about my plans yet." His voice was as bad as the others. Every word had wind in it. "I might even go to sea for a year before I make up my mind about Harvard." False, Daniel told himself. False. Not only the voice now, but the words. He had no notion of going to sea but there was something about Mr. Leonard that made a person want to appear his opposite— unimpressed with education and position. And gold lace. He could see Mr. Leonard exchanging glances with *her*, but instead of inquiring further into his future, a subject Daniel shut out of his mind as much as possible, Mr. Leonard turned to politics.

He reached into his vest pocket, took out a gold snuffbox, shook back the ruffles on his wrist, and inhaled delicately.

"The Whig leaders," he said, "have seen the light, I believe. They're talking conciliation now. I hear that even Mr. Adams may be willing to pay for the tea."

"I should hope so," Mrs. West trilled.

Mr. Leonard nodded, self-assured, like a dog walking away from a bone he has buried. "They tell me there will be no contention at this session."

Dr. West sighed. "That's a blessing."

"The important thing," Mr. Leonard said, settling back against the velvet love seat, "is that we revere the empire."

Daniel thought of the lion and the unicorn and for the first time he smiled at Mr. Leonard.

"There's three thousand miles between us and England," Mr. Leonard said. "It makes governing difficult. We can't expect all the privileges of the parent state."

Daniel leaned forward.

"We have to sacrifice. For the present, even our charter itself, if necessary. And whatever it means, acknowledge Parliament freely as our master."

Daniel decided he had smiled prematurely. The charter itself! That meant really giving up self-government. He waited for Mrs. West and his father to take issue with this last statement but they were nodding in agreement.

Mr. Leonard took another pinch of snuff. "But, as I say, I think the Whigs have heard the whip crack. They're banking their fires."

Indeed, for the first few days the Court did seem quiet. It was a quiet, however, that the people of Salem didn't quite trust and many of them did not even welcome. There was always a crowd around the Town House, urging the Whig representatives to take strong action against what had now become known as the Intolerable Acts.

Then on the sixth day the Court presented an address to General Gage that sent him slamming out of the room right in the middle of the session. Daniel was in the upstairs hall and for the first time had a close look at the governor as he stopped to speak to Secretary Flucker, who had followed him out of the room.

"I will not listen to an insult to any officer of the Crown," General Gage said. Looking at him, Daniel's heart fell. The general did not look like a mediating man. His lips were thin and hard. "I am not here to argue or to reason," he said. "To hear old grudges. Or to make personal judgments. I am here to carry out the king's commands and I intend to do it."

The people stood silent as General Gage swept out of the Town House. Then the door opened again and Mr. Ward, the doorkeeper, stepped out of the room, looking to see if General Gage had really left the building.

"He's left, all right," one of the crowd said as they all moved up to Mr. Ward. "What was that about?"

Mr. Ward raised his hands, palms up, in a gesture of incomprehension. "They didn't say anything against the general," he said. "They were as respectful as you please. All they did was to make some unkind remarks about Governor Hutchison, but who here in Massachusetts isn't used to that? I've heard a heap worse." Shaking his head, Mr. Ward eased himself back into the courtroom.

General Gage didn't go back to court and Mr. Leonard reported that the general wouldn't go back unless there was an apology. He would do what business was needed from his residence. In other words, Daniel thought, General Gage was out of the way. He remembered the conversation between Mr. Paine and Mr. Adams. "If we can get the governor out of the way," Mr. Paine had said, "I can take care of Leonard."

Then on the afternoon of June 16th Mr. Paine came to call at the Wests' home. He was a handsome, carefree, smiling man and even though he was a Whig,

142

Mrs. West played up to him, offering him and Mr. Leonard the doctor's office so they could talk business privately.

Mr. Paine laughed. "But we have nothing private to discuss," he said. "I am not here on business, only as a neighbor. As you may know, Mr. Leonard and I have been neighbors in Taunton for many years. I hope you and your son will stay with us." He nodded in Daniel's direction.

Daniel didn't think he could have gone out of the room if he'd been asked to. He sat on the edge of his chair, waiting—he didn't know for what, but waiting.

"I'm away on government business so much," Mr. Paine said, "that every once in a while I get homesick and long for some Taunton talk." He turned to Mr. Leonard. "I've been thinking all day," he said, "of that cherry orchard behind your house. It must be in full bloom now." He smiled at Mrs. West. "There's nothing like the sight of Mr. Leonard's cherry trees when they're in blossom."

In a few minutes the two men were deep in a discussion of Taunton, re-creating sights and sounds of their home town. The more they talked, the more Mr. Leonard loosened up. Yet for all the innocence of the conversation, Daniel did not move back in his chair. He felt as if he were watching a man lay a trap, baiting it, hiding it behind a screen of grass, covering it carefully with earth, crouching behind a tree, and waiting for the proper moment to spring it.

Suddenly Mr. Paine slapped his knee. "Tomorrow is the opening of the Court in Taunton. Why don't we ride down there for the day? There's nothing of import on the agenda here for the next few days. We wouldn't even be missed."

Daniel found himself half rising from his chair and then he sat down again. He should warn Mr. Leonard, he told himself. He should stand up right now and tell Mr. Leonard not to walk into that trap. The Whigs were up to something.

"My wife is always writing that she wishes I would send her some chocolate," Mr. Paine went on, "and I've found a supply up here in Salem. It would be a good opportunity for me to take it to her."

Daniel's hands tightened on the arms of his chair. Now, he told himself. Now. He waited to hear his voice break into the conversation. Instead, all he heard was Robert Treat Paine talking like a young boy who has suddenly thought up a lark.

Mr. Paine put his hand on Mr. Leonard's shoulder. "Well, Daniel," he said, "now that I've thought about it, I can't resist the idea. I'm going back to Goodhue's, saddle my horse, and start right out." He waited a fraction of a moment. "I hope you'll come with me."

Mr. Leonard hesitated. "What is coming up in the Court here tomorrow, Robert?"

Mr. Paine waved his hand. "Treasury matters, I believe. Routine things. Reports." He turned to Mrs. West. "People don't realize," he said, "how much time their representatives have to give to the simple house-keeping business of a province. Matters that don't involve any controversy at all."

Mr. Leonard fingered the lace on his shirt front.

144

"Yes," he said, "I suppose that will be all. General Gage has made it clear that he'll stand for no nonsense at this session."

"Nonsense?" Mr. Paine raised an eyebrow. "I don't see how there can be, as you say, any nonsense. We're all agreed to that."

"Well, Robert." Mr. Leonard stood up. "It's a temptation. I'll go with you. It will be a holiday."

Daniel stood up too, his hands hanging at his sides, as Robert Treat Paine left the house. Now, he said to himself again. Now was the time. He could stop Mr. Leonard on his way up the stairs to pack his bag. He could say, "Mr. Leonard, I think you should know about a conversation I overheard in the Town House. They want you out of the way." But instead he watched Mr. Leonard climb the full flight of stairs and then as his stepmother went into the kitchen, Daniel walked over to the clock on the mantelpiece and faced the little girl with the upraised arm. "What do you think you're doing?" he snapped. "Your hand always up in the air? You pledging allegiance forever or something?"

When Mr. Leonard came back down the stairs, Daniel turned suddenly toward him. "Mr. Leonard," he said, "don't you think this court should discuss the Intolerable Acts at all?"

"Certainly not," Mr. Leonard replied. "Nor do I think they are necessarily intolerable." He was in a hurry. He went to the kitchen to bid Mrs. West good-bye; then he started for the stable and Daniel followed. The chariot, black and shiny, was standing in the

145

driveway but, for such a quick trip, Mr. Leonard was going to ride. Daniel helped him saddle his horse. He put the bit in the horse's mouth and as Mr. Leonard was getting into the saddle, Daniel spoke again.

"Don't you think," he asked, "that the ruling on the town meetings is very harsh?"

"No." Mr. Leonard adjusted the tails of his coat and ran his hand down the front as if he were making sure that all the lace showed. "Only way to stop the populace from making trouble," he said, "is to see that they don't get together. Obedience, not compromise, is what is in order." He picked up the reins. "Any more questions, Daniel?"

Daniel hesitated. "No," he said at last. "Nothing." He handed Mr. Leonard his bag and waited for him to strap it to his saddle, and then he watched him walk his horse to the corner of Paved Street where he was to meet Mr. Paine.

The next morning Daniel was the first spectator to arrive at the Town House. Most of the representatives were already in the courtroom and only he and Mr. Ward, the doorkeeper, were in the corridor.

"Mr. Adams here yet?" Daniel asked.

Mr. Ward nodded. "Yep. The first one. Always is." He was fingering a big key he held in his hand.

"What's the key for?" Daniel asked.

"As soon as the Court comes to order," Mr. Ward said, "I'm to lock the door. I'm to see that no one goes in or out."

"Have you done this before?"

"Nope. They've never bothered about the door one way or another before this morning."

"Why do you suppose they want the door locked this morning?"

"Who knows?" Mr. Ward shrugged. "I don't pretend to understand the goings-on in there. They say, lock the door, I lock it. They say, open the door, I open it."

Several more representatives were coming down the corridor now—Colonel Elisha Jones, the Tory from Weston, among them. When they were settled in the courtroom, Daniel heard the loud banging of a gavel and then Mr. Adams' voice. "Lock the door, Mr. Ward," he said. And Mr. Ward went into the room and a moment later Daniel heard the key turn in the lock.

He wasn't alone in the corridor long. The usual group of interested people began assembling. One of them asked Daniel if he'd seen Mr. Ward and if the Court was in session yet. When Daniel mentioned that the door was locked, it was as if he'd lighted a spark on a long fuse. The news sizzled through the Town House and before long into the town itself, so that in no time at all the steps were crowded. More than once, Daniel wished he'd kept quiet about that key. He was tense enough about what was going on inside that courtroom, wondering why on earth he'd let Mr. Leonard slip away.

Then all at once the door to the courtroom flew open and out stumbled Colonel Elisha Jones, the Tory. His hands clutched his stomach.

147

Samuel Adams' voice thundered from inside. "Mr. Ward," he said, "your orders were to keep the door locked and not let anyone *in* or *out*. You have let Colonel Jones *out*."

Mr. Ward stood in the doorway. "The gentleman said—" He hesitated. "He said he had to answer a call of nature. I didn't want him to—"

As the door closed and the key turned, the people in the hall let loose with a great roar of laughter. The tension was dissipated but it was clear that the call that Elisha Jones was answering was a call of a political nature. As soon as he was out of the courtroom, he let go of his stomach and, accompanied by an assortment of coarse remarks, he elbowed his way out to the street. He jumped on his horse and galloped away.

"Off to tattle to the governor," the people said. Whatever was brewing in the courtroom, Elisha Jones was trying to stop it.

Over an hour later the door was still locked. Jeremy had heard about the doings and he joined Daniel in the upper corridor, where jokes were being passed back and forth like bad money, all at the expense of Colonel Jones.

Then Secretary Flucker galloped up to the Town House. Under his arm he had a scroll.

"I have orders from the governor," he announced breathlessly and made his way up the stairs. At the sight of the precise and flustered Mr. Flucker, the joking became louder and rougher.

"What's the governor ordering?" someone called. "An inside water closet?"

"No," another voice drawled. "He just sent over some paper."

Daniel and Jeremy, standing against the courtroom door, moved over as Secretary Flucker walked up and knocked on the door. Daniel thought he'd never seen a man look as miserable.

"That's right, Mr. Secretary," a seaman snickered. "Do your duty."

Mr. Flucker's face was scarlet all the way up to his wig but he knocked again. "Open up," he called. "On the orders of His Excellency."

Inside, Mr. Adams' voice could be clearly heard. "Mr. Ward," he cried, "keep that door fast."

Secretary Flucker tried several more times but when it was clear that his knocking was to no purpose, he turned around, unrolled the scroll, and in a loud voice began to read what it said. He was a pretty ridiculous sight, Daniel thought. Shouting high-flown government language at such a raucous crowd. And at the end all it amounted to was that the governor had dissolved the meeting of the General Court which, in spite of any announcement, was still going about its business, whatever it was, inside that closed room.

It was not long after Secretary Flucker had left the building, however, that the courtroom door opened. This time the crowd quieted immediately as Mr. Adams came out of the room. He blinked at the people who packed the hall and then he smiled.

"Gentlemen," he said, "the motion has just been made and carried that a general congress of deputies meet at Philadelphia in the near future to determine wise and proper measures for recovering our just rights and liberties."

He had scarcely finished when a loud huzzah rang out from the upper hall of the Town House.

"A general congress. All the colonies." Jeremy nodded. "That's the way. We can't do it alone. We'll show the king that we aren't just a peculiar, freedom-loving faction here in Massachusetts."

Daniel thought of Mr. Adams' words—"to determine wise and proper measures." Surely this was a step in the right direction, and for the first time he was truly glad that he hadn't stopped Mr. Leonard from going to Taunton.

When he got home, he found that his father, who had been complaining of a sore knee for the last few days, was sick with the gout. He was in bed the next day when Mr. Leonard returned from Taunton, furious at what had happened in his absence and in a hurry to turn around and leave again, now that the Court had adjourned. His chariot had to be hitched, his bags brought down, food prepared, and fresh water had to be pumped for a pitcher so Mr. Leonard could wash up.

When he was finally ready to go, Daniel went up with him to Dr. West's room to say good-bye.

"Well, Doctor," Mr. Leonard said, "our visit which began so happily did not end up well for either of us, did it?"

The room smelled of camphor oil.

"About the only good it accomplished was for Daniel," Mr. Leonard said.

"I want to thank you for that." Dr. West smiled.

Daniel put his hand on the bedpost, but before he could ask what they were talking about, the conversation was over. Dr. West closed his eyes as if he were in pain and Mr. Leonard said a quick good-bye and left the room.

Later, however, after Mr. Leonard had left, Daniel asked his stepmother about the conversation.

Mrs. West raised her eyebrows. "What did your father say?"

"He thanked Mr. Leonard for something. He didn't say any more."

"Then I guess there's nothing more to know. And the way your father is feeling, I wouldn't bother him."

Daniel certainly wasn't going to beg for information.

Chapter Ten

D<small>R. W<small>EST</small>'S GOUT</small> turned out to be a long and pain-
ful attack and Daniel's time was taken up with
helping to care for him. Even when he could get out
of bed, the doctor needed help. Unable to go out on
sick calls, the doctor hobbled into his office late every
afternoon when school was out, propped his leg on a
chair and saw patients there. But someone had to be

with him to open the door when the bell rang, to hand him equipment or medication, and even, under his instruction, to put on bandages or treat wounds.

"You think you'd like to be a doctor, Daniel?" Dr. West asked the day after Daniel had bandaged the arm of a child who had been burned.

"No, sir," Daniel said. "I'm sorry. I don't feel any inclinations in that direction at all."

"What direction do you feel your inclinations?"

"I don't know."

Dr. West sighed and touched his sore knee. "You should be knowing by now, Daniel. I haven't mentioned it because until recently our household has been so upset. But we're on an even keel now. We're back to normal."

Normal! Daniel drew in his breath. How could anyone think this was normal? His father hadn't even tried to do the things that Daniel considered normal—none of the things they used to do. Not once, for instance, had he even mentioned fishing.

"I'm on the mend now," Dr. West went on. "You won't need to help me much longer."

"You think you'll be out and walking soon, do you?"

Dr. West nodded. "In a few days. As good as new."

Daniel fingered a bottle of camphor oil. "Think you'd be up to going fishing sometime?"

When Daniel looked at his father, he knew he wasn't thinking about fishing. "You're changing the subject, Daniel," Dr. West said. "We were talking about your future. I've been hoping you'd come to me about it."

Daniel returned his attention to the bottle in his hand. "Give me some more time," he mumbled.

"Well, I'll wait, but time is what you're running out of, Daniel."

During the summer Daniel often thought of what his father had said about time. He made time sound as if it were nothing more than sand trickling through an hourglass, a certain number of grains and each grain the same size and weight as the grain before, the present and future slipping effortlessly into the past. But time wasn't like that, Daniel thought. Most of the summer did trickle by, one day no different from the others, but on some days time seemed to get lumped up and pass through that narrowing in the glass with the greatest difficulty. It was hard to think about the future when time behaved like that.

There were two days in particular that summer that Daniel found difficult. The first day was the Fast Day proclaimed on July fourteenth to protest the Port Bill. People were not supposed to eat all day. Instead they were to send the food they would have eaten to the needy in Boston. In the West home, however, Hannah was ordered to prepare food as usual.

"If the people in Boston are hungry," Mrs. West said, "it is their own fault. Let John Adams feed them."

At school the Whig boys made a great show of being noble and strong in spite of their empty stomachs.

"I suppose you're going home to a feast of roast beef and mashed potatoes," Benjie had snarled at Beckett and Daniel.

"Yea," Thomas Clark chimed in. "And you'll eat off a *lace* tablecloth."

Beckett and Daniel walked silently while behind them the Whigs shouted the names of all the delicacies they could think of. "Plum pudding!" they cried. "Mince pie! Turtle soup!" In a flash or inspiration, Benjie added, "Snails! Fresh from France!" and the Whigs laughed, breaking up now to go their separate ways, calling advice back and forth to each other on how to avoid fainting from weakness. When the time came to eat that night, Daniel had difficulty swallowing. He tried not to think of the hungering people in Boston, but in spite of himself, the mashed potatoes stuck in his throat.

The second difficult day was August thirteenth. A fleet of transports from Boston sailed into Salem Harbor that day and the 59th Regiment of regulars landed on Winter Island. Every boy in town walked out to the Neck and watched the soldiers make camp. Daniel told himself that this was even more exciting than a parade or a muster but when he stood on the causeway that led to the island, he didn't feel the way he had expected. Winter Island was a haven for fishermen and picknickers and here it was, covered with redcoats. Some of them were making camp right at the spot where Daniel and his father had been accustomed to drop their lines; others were tramping over the best picnic places. They were shouting back and forth, moving guns and ammunition, chopping down trees when it suited them. Some of them came to the end of the causeway and stared at the crowd assembled as if they were natives who had to be subdued.

"They don't look any friendlier than the ones in Boston," one soldier remarked loudly.

Daniel didn't stay on the causeway long. Still, there was no forgetting the soldiers. They came into town on their time off, poking into stores and taverns as if they owned the place. They were well enough behaved (they were not even allowed to wear side arms into Salem for fear of provoking the populace) but they had that air about them as if they could scarcely wait to clean up the country and get out. Moreover, they had constantly to make themselves heard. Their bugles were the first thing Salem heard in the morning and the last thing it heard at night. Even on Sunday.

Daniel always enjoyed Sunday morning. Before getting up, he'd lie in bed awhile and listen to the church bells. There was the deep, solemn bass ring of St. Peter's close by, and in the distance, the fainter, higher, more modest peal of the bells in the East Church near the waterfront. They talked to each other, those bells, in the still morning, in that perfect hour when only nature is awake and birds are astir, before people begin mixing in and churning about. Over the sleeping houses the bells talked, Daniel thought, about the calm things of the world—the quiet flow of a river, the slow, persistent growth of a seed, the pattern of the stars.

But on the Sunday after the regiment arrived, the bells had hardly started before the bugle from Winter Island butted in. Shrill and commanding, the bugle didn't give a hang for stars or seeds. It didn't give a hang for the future or for a person who was trying to settle his mind. All it wanted was to whip the world along faster *now*; it wouldn't listen to the bells at all.

Daniel got up and went grumpily down to breakfast. Everyone was at the kitchen table.

"Did you hear that bugle?" Daniel asked. "Busting in on the church bells! It made me sick."

Mrs. West looked surprised. "Why, I *love* that bugle," she said. "Every time I hear it, I feel safe. I'm just so grateful for those boys on Winter Island."

Daniel glared at his stepmother. He had disliked her before but never, he thought, as much as at this moment. He helped himself to another of Hannah's hotcakes and tried to pretend his stepmother wasn't there.

Then suddenly Mrs. West put her napkin down beside her plate. It was the final way she put it down that attracted Daniel's attention. She leaned over and spoke to her husband. "We can't put off talking to Daniel any longer," she said. "Why don't you tell him?"

"Tell me what?" Daniel asked. He didn't really want to know. Whatever it was, he was sure it wasn't good and certainly his father didn't look happy. On the other hand, he gave no indication that he was trying to avoid the conversation.

"Yes, it's appropriate," he agreed. He turned to Daniel. "Well, Daniel," he said, "I told you once that time was running out for you. Your mother is right. It's run out now. And we've made some plans for you."

157

Daniel put down his fork.

"As you know," Dr. West said, "we haven't been at all satisfied with the preparation Mr. Nicholls is giving you. We'd like you to attend another school for a year."

Was that all? Daniel thought. That was no catastrophe. He didn't in the least mind leaving Mr. Nicholls' beehive.

"Mr. Leonard told us of a very fine school," Dr. West went on, "and he has kindly written a letter of introduction for you."

"Yes?" Daniel recalled his father's conversation with Mr. Leonard. "Fine." He went back to his breakfast.

"It's going to be a great expense," Dr. West said, "but your mother wants to finance it."

Slowly Daniel raised his eyes. "Where is this school?" he asked.

Dr. West cleared his throat. "In England. Not far from London."

"England!" Daniel looked around the table at the circle of hopeful faces in league against him. It was a family that had united behind his back. *He* was the misfit, the only one who wasn't pleased with the present arrangement of the household, he thought. And now they wanted him to go. Even his father wanted him to go. Daniel pushed himself away from the table.

"Think it over, Daniel," Dr. West said. "You can continue meanwhile at Mr. Nicholls' summer session. The ship you'll be going on doesn't leave for another six weeks."

They had even made arrangements for his transportation. Daniel rushed out of the house. He didn't know where he was bound for but he found himself after a while at the end of Derby Wharf, breathless, staring straight out to sea. Toward England.

"I won't go," he said. "I won't go."

For weeks he'd got by without falling into a grief hole, but now he'd fallen and he'd hit bottom. Glumly he looked over at Winter Island, where even from here he could see a clump of redcoats. To go where those soldiers came from! he thought. Where people couldn't understand how someone loyal to the king would still want his freedom!

He sat down on the dock with his head between his knees and listened to the gulls screech overhead. Someone on the island started to beat a drum. A steady, monotonous, negative beat as if the person had come upon the word "no" and couldn't let it go. Daniel put his fingers in his ears. It didn't drown out the sound but it dulled it. He knew there were footsteps behind him but they were like an echo to the drum. He was vaguely aware when the echo stopped but he didn't look up until a voice spoke.

"Don't care much for the drums, I see," the voice said.

Daniel took his fingers out of his ears. There was a British soldier sitting on a barrel a few feet away from him. He was a jaunty, dark-haired young man with a teasing look about him, but all Daniel could see was the red coat. He grunted and shifted his position.

"Can't stand the sight of me, can you, Yankee?" The

soldier chuckled. "You people! You see us and you pretend we're not there. You hear us and you put your fingers in your ears. Hate us, don't you?"

"We don't all hate you," Daniel grumbled, not looking at the soldier. "My stepmother *loves* you, if that's any comfort. She *dotes* on the sound of your bugle. You make her feel *safe*."

The soldier laughed. "So you have a stepmother, do you, Yankee? Now we're getting somewhere." He had his legs spread apart and he rapped his knuckles on the barrel between his knees. "I take it your stepmother is not to your liking. She's a Tory, I suppose."

Daniel stared out to sea. "We're a Tory family."

"All but you. You're the renegade. You're the black sheep, is that it, Yankee? Down here on the dock with your fingers in your ears and a storm on your face."

"I'm a Tory too."

The soldier whistled and rapped on the barrel. "You? If you call yourself loyal, I don't know what you'd call me."

"I could find words."

"I'm sure you could," the soldier grinned, "but I don't know as I care to hear them. I'd rather talk about you. The boy who hates British soldiers. Yet calls himself a Tory."

Daniel shifted his position.

"On what grounds do you claim to be a Tory?"

"On the usual grounds," Daniel snapped. "I'm for going along with unjust laws and trying to settle them peacefully. I revere the empire. You want me to swear allegiance or something?"

"No. No. Any patriot is still willing to do that. But settling peacefully? It's all settled, Yankee. The king isn't going to listen any more. He isn't going to let you talk. Not even in town meetings." The soldier rapped one, two, three on the barrel. "So *if* you're a Tory, *if* you uphold peace as you contend, there's only one thing left you can do. You bend your knee. 'All right, Your Majesty,' you say. 'You know best, Your Majesty.' Well, Yankee," he laughed, "is that what you say?"

Daniel jumped to his feet, his back against the piling. "Stop calling me Yankee," he shouted. "And stop that —that"—he pointed to the barrel—"that infernal tapping."

The soldier grinned and folded his arms across his chest. "All I want to do is to establish facts. And that brings me to a very pertinent fact. I see you're going to have a town meeting right here in Salem, no matter what the king or anyone says. Is that right?"

"Well, there's going to be a meeting."

"August 24th. I saw the notice posted. You go along with that?"

Daniel knew that Jeremy was worried about the meeting. He knew how carefully the notice had been worded so that it couldn't be called an official meeting. "It's not really a town meeting," Daniel explained. "The selectmen didn't call it. It's the Committee of Correspondence that called it. That makes it different. Besides, it's only to elect delegates to a county meeting in Ipswich. And no one ever forbade a county meeting."

The soldier threw back his head and laughed. "That's good Whig reasoning, all right."

"Well, people have to *talk!*" Daniel shouted.

"And you'd be the last one to stop them, wouldn't you?" The soldier smiled. "If you had it in your power, you might even reason your way into helping the Whigs find the opportunity to talk."

Daniel thought of how he'd let Mr. Leonard slip off when the Continental Congress was being planned. "You've heard of self-government, I suppose," he said coldly.

"Oh yes, I've heard of it. I even enjoy it. To a degree. Only I'm not so cocky about it. I don't have an ocean to hide behind."

"The ocean is what makes governing difficult."

The man spread his hands out, palms up. "There you go," he said. "Blaming the ocean."

He was insufferable, Daniel thought. Now he was slapping his belt, where his side arms usually hung. "Well, the talking days and the reasoning days will soon be over," he said. "Maybe sooner than you think." Suddenly he leaned toward Daniel. "Why don't we play a little game, you and I? A supposing game. We'll start supposing the governor calls out the troops to stop the town meeting. Then supposing the town resists the troops and supposing you find yourself on the sidelines."

"I'm not supposing."

"But it's your turn to suppose!" The soldier stood up and looked at Daniel until Daniel was forced to

162

meet his eyes. "Which side will you cheer for?" he asked. "The troops or the town?"

Daniel knew very well which side he'd cheer for and he didn't care for the game.

"Those are the only choices you've got now, Yankee. Either you're for freedom first and let the empire fry. Or else you're for the empire the whole way. I know. I just came from England. And I wasn't sent here to talk."

Daniel started to walk down the dock, but the soldier fell in step beside him.

"Of course," the soldier added, "there is a third choice. A lot of Tories are taking it. You *could* go to England. *If* you're a Tory, you'd be welcome."

"I'm not going to England!" Daniel broke into a run. The soldier didn't try to go with him. Only his laughter followed. "Never mind, Yankee," he called. "At your age it doesn't matter what you are. At least not yet."

Daniel went into the Common. If he walked fast enough and far enough, he figured, he'd get that soldier's face out of his mind. He'd put that laughter behind him. He went past Flag Pond and Mason's Pond and Cheevers Pond, all the way to the Almshouse, where he had to slow down to catch his breath.

Two old men were sitting on the steps of the Almshouse, blinking at the sun, telling each other how the difficulties with England should be settled. Pulling at their pipes, they were talking slowly and leisurely, grazing over a field of thought, unmindful that there might not be a right way to settle things any longer.

Daniel hurried by, making his way to the North River, then following it upstream, past the drawbridge and into open country. Somewhere along the river he left the soldier behind. He couldn't even remember what he looked like and when he tried to recall his voice, he discovered that the soldier's voice had become his own voice and the soldier's questions were questions Daniel was asking himself. "If you're not a Tory, Daniel West," he asked himself at last, "what are you?"

But although he stayed beside the river all afternoon, Daniel couldn't bring himself to answer that final question. He couldn't say the word. Nor was it necessary, he told himself. Scuffing up the riverbank, thrashing thoughts back and forth, he'd found other answers to satisfy his father.

It was almost dark when he got home. Dr. and Mrs. West were sitting in the kitchen when Daniel walked in.

"You've been away a long time," Dr. West said.

"Yes, it's been a long time." Daniel leaned against the door, more tired than he ever remembered. He didn't look at his stepmother. She had nothing to do with what he had to say.

"You left us rather abruptly this morning," Dr. West said.

"I've been walking." Daniel talked as though he were still out of breath. "And thinking," he added.

"Yes?"

"About my future. You're always asking me about it."

Dr. West leaned forward.

"A person can hardly keep his future these days separated from the future of the country." He took a deep breath. At the river when he'd planned what he would say, it had seemed easier. He'd thought ahead to a time when the country might again map its course the right way, when it wouldn't be left with only two wrong ways, when talking could make a difference. But now with his father leaning forward so anxiously, with his stepmother making little cross-stitches on the piece of embroidery in her lap, he couldn't find the words.

"I'll be a lawyer," he said shortly. "And I'll go to Philadelphia to study. Or Virginia. Or Boston." He walked over to the sink and dipped himself a cup of water from the bucket that stood there. "But I won't go to England."

Dr. West leaned back in his chair. "The law is a fine profession, Daniel," he said slowly. "I'm pleased you've made a decision. But the best training for the law is in England. The state the country is in, you might not finish even a year of schooling here."

"I'll take my chances." Daniel drank the water, which was warm from standing in the house all day.

Dr. West shook his head. "It's not just the schooling. Things are working up to a climax in this country. We want to get you away from it."

Daniel swung around to face his father, who was standing now too. "That's all you want. To get me away."

165

"You know better than that." Dr. West's eyes didn't leave Daniel's face. "England is the only place for a young man with loyal sympathies."

Daniel put his hands on the back of a chair to steady himself. "Maybe I'm not loyal," he said.

For a moment it was very quiet in the kitchen. Dr. West exchanged a quick glance with his wife and she put aside her embroidery.

"You're just wrought up, Daniel," she said. "You must be hungry." She got up and went to the pantry for a plate of cold chicken. "You'll feel better when you get something in your stomach." She talked as if Daniel were a small child with a fever and what he really needed was a dose of salts. "It doesn't matter, does it," she said sweetly, "what the political opinions of a fourteen-year-old are?"

"Fifteen next month," Daniel interrupted. "Some places they take fifteen-year-olds in the militia."

"Fourteen or fifteen," Mrs. West said, "it's of no import. And we don't want to hear any more about the militia." She fixed a place at the table. "You've just been listening to too much liberty talk. You'll feel differently when you're in England. Now come and eat."

Daniel sat down. His father put his hand on Daniel's shoulder. "You'll get used to the idea. Mr. Derby's *Quero* on which you'll be sailing doesn't leave until October."

"I won't be on it." Daniel's voice was shaking. "I'm no longer a Tory, I tell you. I'm not for obedience."

It was as if he hadn't spoken. They acted as if his

166

beliefs were a notion he'd picked up at the Common, a whim he was following just to keep in style. They seemed to think it was easy for him to change his loyalties. But nothing about it was easy. He knew now he'd been working up to the change for some time, but although he admitted to not being a Tory, he still couldn't say what he was. He couldn't bring himself to use the word. And when he went to bed that night, he thought of the lion and the unicorn that he'd relegated to second place. He thought of the pride he'd taken in seeing them on the wall of the Town House, guarding not only his life, he'd thought, but his freedom as well. He closed his eyes. This was a new grief hole and he guessed it would take a while to climb out of it.

Chapter Eleven

JEREMY WASN'T at all surprised about Daniel's change of loyalties. He'd seen it coming, he said, and understood how hard it was to make such a change. But Daniel wanted the grieving to be over before he told others. He wanted to do it in a wholehearted way, taking pride in his convictions as Jeremy did, showing confidence in the future. He wanted to come right out and use the word he'd been avoiding, the word he'd always pronounced with such contempt. *Whig*—he and Beckett had blown the word out as if the very air in it were foul.

He'd have to tell Beckett. The thought was a coldness inside him. He tried out different speeches but it was as if it were someone else talking. How could he tell Beckett he was deserting a cause they'd upheld together, lying on pine cones at Ding-Dong Allison's, crouching in the darkness on Gallows Hill, a cause they'd upheld through taunts and insults and opposition?

The day of the town meeting came and still Daniel hadn't told but he promised himself that at the noon recess, when the meeting would be either over or called off, he'd tell—Beckett first and later in the day he'd tell Charlie and Benjie. With school in session, there would be no opportunity to go to the Town House and watch what went on, but people didn't expect trouble. The governor was reported to be angry but he'd done nothing to stop the meeting and no one supposed he would now.

It rained the morning of the meeting, one of those long, hard rains determined, it seems, to turn the land back over to the sea. Rivers of water rushed down the streets, sheets of water cascaded down roofs, walls of water flung themselves so fiercely at Daniel and Beckett on the way to school that there was no opportunity to talk about the town meeting or anything else. When they finally got into the schoolroom, they found themselves alone except for Mr. Nicholls, who remarked rather testily that although he'd been able to get to school on time, he supposed the rain was delaying the others. But as time went on, it became clear that the others weren't coming and Daniel knew it wasn't because of the rain. They were playing hooky. Perhaps they'd heard something new concerning the town meeting; Charlie's father was, after all, a Committee member.

With the classroom all but empty, Daniel took a seat by the window instead of his customary one in the middle of the room, thinking that he might see activity of some kind that would give him a hint of what was going on. The ledge of the window, however, was so high he couldn't see the street unless he stood up. He waited until Mr. Nicholls seemed absorbed in his droning and carefully he raised up and looked out. Only rain; nothing more. It was after he'd stood up the third time that Mr. Nicholls slammed down his book.

"Since you're determined to be on your feet, Daniel West," he said, "you can stay there and translate the next passage for us."

Daniel picked up his book but before looking at it, he took another quick glance outside and it was then he saw Mr. Carver, one of the most hotheaded of the local Whigs. He was running through the rain and he held a gun in his hand.

"We're waiting," Mr. Nicholls said.

The passage was from Cicero's first oration against Cataline. Daniel tried to put his mind to it. "What an age is ours!" he read. "You are attacking our whole

170

constitution." He looked out the window. Mr. Carver was out of sight. "And our immortal gods," he went on. He stumbled and hesitated. "The houses of our city and the lives of our citizens." He glanced up again but when he looked back, he'd lost his place.

"It seems," Mr. Nicholls said icily, "that not only are five of our members physically absent, a sixth one might as well not be here. For tomorrow I assign you a double translation. To be written out. As for now, it hardly seems profitable to continue. Class is dismissed." He'd barely finished his words when he was out of the room and Daniel and Beckett were left alone.

"What did you see?" Beckett asked.

Daniel went to the window. "Mr. Carver. He had a gun in his hand."

"Headed toward the Town House?"

"Yes." There was no avoiding it, Daniel thought. He'd have to tell Beckett now. They couldn't go to the Town House together with Beckett thinking that they shared the same views and that things were the same as always. He went to the hook for his coat.

"Beckett," he said slowly, "what do you think of the Committee calling this town meeting?"

"What do you suppose I think?" Beckett was bent over, adjusting his boots. "It was a mistake. Right from the beginning. If there's trouble, it's their doing."

"You go along with the ordinance against the town meetings?"

"I don't like it but I go along. Of course I go along. It's the king's orders. And I'm his subject. Every time

171

folks differ, they can't take things into their own hands."

"Right or wrong, you go along with anything the king says?"

"I may disagree but then maybe the king knows more than I do." Beckett straightened. "Yes, I go along. Right or wrong, I'm with the king and Parliament. And so are you, Daniel West, so stop your foolishness."

"Sometimes I put right before the king. If the right is big enough." Daniel's voice sounded small, not proud the way he'd meant it to. He had one arm in his coat; he let the other sleeve dangle. "I've come around to putting freedom before the empire." He watched Beckett lower himself into one of the classroom seats. "We have to have meetings. We have to have a say in how our lives are run. We have to talk as long as talking's possible. And if that doesn't work and if there's no other way—"

"What?"

Daniel felt himself cringing, his back up against a wall. "If they start to fight, we'll have to fight."

Beckett's face was unbelieving. "You're not trying to tell me, are you, that you've *turned*?"

Daniel winced. "I've changed. I'm a—" He stopped and then started the sentence again. "I'm no longer a Tory."

"Well." Beckett's hands lay loosely on his knees. He stared down at the floor.

"We've always said we respected other people's opinions even if they differ from ours. We've always said we didn't see why politics should interfere with friendship."

"Yes, that's what we've said." Beckett didn't look up.

"I don't want things to change between us, Beckett."

"Well." Beckett kept studying the floor. "You've got a right to change, I guess. I'll get used to it. I don't hold it against you." For the first time Beckett looked up. His face was miserable. "It's not *me* that's going to come between us, Daniel. It's *them*. They'll try to turn you against me."

Daniel thrust his arm into the sleeve of his coat. "Well, they won't succeed."

"You're going to tell them—Benjie and the rest?"

"Yes. Today."

Beckett got up and put on his coat. He set his hat on his head—straight, not pushed back the way he normally wore it. "I suppose you're going to the Town House now."

"Yes."

"And watch Tom Carver and maybe a lot of other hotheads wave their guns around?"

Daniel didn't reply.

"I guess I'll go down to the harbor to see how the boat's making out in the storm."

They walked together to the door. Beckett put his hand on the latch and then he hesitated. He took a deep breath and let it out slowly. "We just won't talk politics, Daniel. There are other things to talk about. Why don't you come over tonight if you've a mind to?"

"I will. I'd like to."

Beckett opened the door and a gust of wind blew the rain in their faces. Daniel put his coat collar up and started toward the Town House while Beckett, seeking to avoid the Town House altogether, took another way. As long as Beckett was in sight, Daniel held himself down to a walk but once he'd turned the corner, he broke into a run.

Town House Square was filled with people running for cover against the rain. In every doorway people were seeking shelter. Daniel ran under the eaves of the saddlemaker's shop. He looked toward the Town House. A few men were coming out the door; a few others were talking on the steps in the rain and several had muskets over their shoulders. But they didn't seem to be adopting any position of alertness or stationing themselves as if they were waiting for trouble.

"It's all over, boy." It was John Morris, the saddlemaker, standing in the door behind Daniel. "You heard?"

"No." Daniel kept his eyes on the Town House.

"The general called the Committee together. About eight o'clock this morning. Ordered them to call off the meeting. They wouldn't do it so he called out the troops. Issued ammunition. Got them on the march." He leaned over and pointed to King Street. "Step out and take a look. You'll see them."

Daniel stepped out where the view was clear. In the distance the lines of redcoats were halted. He stepped back into the doorway.

"That's as far as they got." The saddlemaker chuckled. "That's when they heard the meeting was over and the delegates elected. Quickest meeting Salem ever had." He paused to savor the event and then went on with even more enjoyment. "And now those pretty redcoats—" He laughed. "All they can do is go back to the Island and dry out." He tapped Daniel on the shoulder. "If you've never seen a wet regiment, boy, now's your opportunity."

Daniel ducked his head into his collar and with his shoulders hunched against the downpour, he made his way down King Street. It was the first time he'd seen the soldiers all together as a regiment, not simply as individual eyesores on the landscape. They were faced toward the Neck, in a double line, obviously waiting for the order to march. Their bayonets were pointed at the sky, their cartridge boxes dangled at their belts, their eyes were straight ahead, unseeing, unfeeling, uncaring. It wasn't like watching a muster or a drill. These soldiers had come into town, Daniel told himself, on a real mission, ready to fire. They were the enemy. And there were more regiments in Boston. More on the way, Daniel had heard. And an empire behind them. Daniel shuddered. How could anyone feel hopeful? How could anyone feel strong?

He was turning to go home when there came from among the ranks a noise that resembled a whistle. Again it came. Faint but distinctly a whistle. Daniel looked but at first he couldn't trace the sound. Then about five rows back from where he was standing,

175

Daniel saw the soldier who had been on the dock. The soldier glanced neither to the right nor the left. His face was immobile, but he was whistling through his teeth. Very softly. His eyes bright with laughter, he was whistling a line of "Yankee Doodle." He didn't need to talk. "It's not over, Yankee," his eyes said. "I'm still here and I wasn't sent to talk."

Suddenly without realizing what he was going to do, Daniel thrust his chin over his upturned collar. He cupped his hands over his mouth. "Lobsterback!" he shouted.

But, of course, the soldier was right. Nothing was over—not even the issue of the town meeting, as it turned out. After the troops went back to the island, the governor was in a towering rage and ordered Peter Frye, the high sheriff, to arrest the Committee members. And that brought the people out again. More of them and angrier than ever. Tom Carver said he'd personally take care of anyone who tried to put a Committee member behind the bars, so although Peter Frye issued the warrants, he was afraid to make any arrests. And now it was rumored that the governor threatened to put the Committee members on board the *Scarborough,* the man-of-war anchored in Boston harbor. He wanted to send them to England as prisoners.

Daniel was at Jeremy's when all this took place and it was Jeremy who came home and reported the doings. He stepped out of his wet boots, walked to the fire, sat down, and held up his stockinged feet to dry. "I wouldn't want to be Peter Frye tonight," he said, shaking his head. "No siree. Not in this town. Nor any Tory, as a matter of fact. Not with the rumors that are flying around here. Tell your folks not to go out on the street tonight, boy. Don't you go out either."

Daniel didn't say anything but he knew he'd go out. He had to see Beckett or he'd think their friendship was already faltering. "I can always tell anyone I'm no longer a Tory," he said.

"It's your father's politics that's going to interest folks, I'm afraid. It was bad enough when he signed that address to Governor Hutchison but why did he have to take Daniel Leonard in as a house guest? Your father and Mr. Foote and Peter Frye and a handful of others, they're considered undesirables. It's thought they might help the governor with his schemes."

"You know my father values peace too much to take an active hand in anything like that."

"I know it but others don't." Jeremy stared at the fire. "Someone might question him. He hasn't modified his views, I suppose?"

"Not a whit. He doesn't talk much. Sometimes it seems he doesn't talk unless he has to, but when he does, he says what he means. And he's as strong a Tory as ever."

Jeremy nodded. "That's what I fear."

"Well, you wouldn't want him to sail under false colors."

"No."

Daniel got up to go. He had his own colors to get out in the open. He'd told Beckett but there were still

177

Benjie and Charlie to tell. He hadn't seen them all day so he went directly to their homes—Charlie's first and Benjie's, but there was no one at either place. The rain had stopped now and the sun was out, making the world hazy with steam. It rose from the hot ground like the last smoke from an old fire or the new smoke from a fresh fire. Daniel cut across the Common, skirting Cheevers Pond, so swollen with rain that the trees around it stood ankle-deep in water. They had an uncomfortable look about them, as if they'd like to shake off the water and step out onto dry land where they belonged. Even the Liberty Boys' oak tree, as if it didn't suffer enough indignities, had water around its base. Daniel stopped at the tree, remembering the day he and Beckett had discovered that first note. He laid his hand on the bark. He was alone now. He was on the same side as the Liberty Boys. And it only made him dislike them more. Still, he knew what some folks said. If it came right down to fighting an empire, they said, you couldn't be choosy about the company you kept. You'd need all the help you could get. Daniel swallowed and put his hand into the hole. The note that he found had today's date on it.

The men are going calling tonight, the note said. *Keep your feathers handy. Then we'll rock the Tory church.*

Daniel didn't know what all of it meant but he felt his anger rising as it always had. He didn't put the note back in the tree. He put it in his pocket.

It was still there when he went to see Beckett. He

went right after supper. He glanced at the sun. Still a couple of daylight hours left, he figured, and he'd get home before dark.

The Footes were assembled in the kitchen when Daniel stepped in the open door. Mrs. Foote was cleaning up the supper dishes. Her sister, Miss Emily, who lived with them, was at the counter polishing glass chimneys of the lamps. Mr. Foote and Beckett were sitting on chairs draped with wet clothes drying before the fire. They were working on old strands of boat rope. Coils of rope lay at their feet. And they were talking about the town meeting.

Daniel stood still, feeling like a stranger, waiting for them to notice him. When they did, they did it all at once. They stopped what they were doing and welcomed him as if he'd been away a long time. Then Beckett pulled out a chair and Daniel felt worse than ever. They were making a show of their friendship. Daniel had come and gone in that kitchen with folks barely looking up and then maybe only to ask him if he'd wiped his feet. Beckett had never pulled a chair out for him in his life.

Daniel sat down. "I see you're lashing," he said. "Could you use another hand?"

Once they were all at work, Daniel felt better. Binding up the rough edges of the rope fiber, they talked about boats and fishing. They planned trips way into the future as if they held the future in their hands. Beckett got out a piece of paper and drew a map of the Misery Islands. This is where they'd make camp, he said, and he marked an *x* on the spot. He drew the cove where they would anchor; he put down a hump for High Point, where they'd go for a view of Salem, and he made a dotted line to show the path at low tide between Big Misery and Little Misery. It was as if there were no differences between them at all. Daniel looked out the window once and saw that it was darkening. When he and Beckett were younger, they'd been allowed to stay out until they could count three stars but Daniel didn't count the stars. He watched Miss Emily light the lamps and delayed his leaving until he couldn't delay it any longer. He put on his coat and fingered his hat. The awkwardness was back; he had to warn them. He looked down at the floor. "Jeremy says that Tories shouldn't go out tonight."

It was then the knocking came at the front door. Behind the knock, there were men's voices.

Mr. Foote's hands went slack at the rope. In Salem people didn't go to a person's front door at night unless there was trouble or a formal gathering. Neighbors went to the back door.

"It's the Whigs," Miss Emily whispered and Daniel remembered the note in his pocket. "The men are going calling tonight."

The Footes were all up now and Mr. Foote was leading the way to the front of the house. Daniel started for the back door but Beckett put his hand on Daniel's arm, stopping him, reassuring him, keeping him in the family group, no matter what was going to take place.

Mr. Foote had the lamp in his hand and while the others stayed in the shadows in the hall, he opened the door. The light fell on four men, members of the Committee of Correspondence. Mr. Sprague was in the front, the spokesman evidently, and behind the four men were gathered a large crowd of people, some of whom Daniel knew and many he didn't recognize— onlookers, men and boys, respectable Whigs and not so respectable. Mr. Foote raised his lamp and Daniel saw Samuel White and Edward Pine. He saw Tom Carver. He didn't have his gun now; he had a club.

As soon as Mr. Sprague started to speak, the crowd quieted. "Good evening," he said. "We don't like to disturb you, Mr. Foote, but we have a rather urgent request to make and we'd be obliged for your signature."

It seemed to Daniel that Mr. Foote's back filled the whole doorway. "I don't give my signature readily," he said, "but if you four gentlemen wish to step in, you may state your business."

He stepped to one side and as the Committee members came in the door, someone in the crowd shouted, "Tar and feathers! Tar and feathers to stubborn Tories!"

Daniel had his hat in his hand. He squeezed it into shapelessness. Those were the people out there he'd aligned himself with. How could he feel proud?

The door closed but although Mr. Foote led the men into the parlor and although Miss Emily brought another lamp, no one sat down.

181

"We have just come from Peter Frye's house," Mr. Sprague explained. "He has most sensibly signed a statement, apologizing for issuing warrants of arrest this morning and renouncing any office, present or future, with the government."

Mr. Foote folded his arms over his chest. "Well?"

"You have less to renounce," Mr. Sprague said, "so it should come easy. You signed an address of welcome to General Gage. And another address to Governor Hutchison. All we want is for you to admit publicly that it was imprudent on your part."

"Whether I regret it or not?"

"We hope you regret it."

"That's all?" There was mockery in Mr. Foote's voice.

"We want you to agree to give no aid to the governor and state that you are a sincere friend of the country."

"I have always been a sincere friend of the country."

"In your lights. Not in ours. We have made it clear in our statement that your convictions have altered." Mr. Sprague spread his hands while through the window the cry of "Tar and Feathers" rang again. "You can see for yourself. After today there's no room in Salem for both Whigs and Tories. We'll get nowhere if there's anyone in town willing to help put our Committee on the *Scarborough*."

"And the alternatives?"

Mr. Sprague glanced uneasily at the other Committee members, who were shifting their weight, holding their hats in their hands. "There are several alternatives," Mr. Sprague finally said. "You can take your chances with the crowd out there. Someone in that crowd, I don't know who, has already fired a shot tonight at the door of General Gage's headquarters in Danvers." He took a deep breath. "For the sake of your family, I beg you not to take that chance. On the other hand, you will have no trouble if you agree to leave Salem tomorrow. The *Neptune* is departing for Halifax in the morning."

The cries outside were becoming louder. Inside, the lamp on the table set tongues of light leaping into the faces of the five men. Mr. Sprague put a piece of paper down on the table and suddenly there seemed to be nothing in the room but that white paper on the cherry table. Everyone looked at it as if they half expected it to take some action on its own. Mr. Foote raised his head first. His eyes sought Mrs. Foote, who was standing behind the Committee members. Then they went to Beckett. No one moved. No one spoke but the Footes had never needed to speak to reach an agreement and before Mr. Foote leaned down to pick up the paper, Daniel knew what the decision was, what it had to be, the Footes being the kind of people they were.

Mr. Foote held the paper in his hand a moment and then with a sudden fierce movement he crumpled it. "*That* for your blasted paper!" he said. "I've never lowered my sails for anyone. And I don't aim to start now." He went to the door and opened it. "If I can't be loyal to the king in Salem, I'll be loyal to him in

Halifax, but loyal I'll be. We'll be on the *Neptune* in the morning. But, gentlemen, you'll see. The governor will win out. I won't be away long."

The Committee members left the house and for a moment the Foote family simply stood and looked at each other. Daniel longed to tell them how proud he was that they had flown their banner so high, no matter that the banner was not the same as his. But already the Footes were leaping ahead to the next step, discussing what they should take with them, what they should leave behind.

Miss Emily stepped out of the shadow. "Don't take the valuables," she said. "I'm not going. No one is going to bother a single lady alone. I'm no political threat. If I stay, the house will be safer. And I will be happier."

Suddenly what had happened struck Daniel with fresh force. Beckett was leaving. And no matter how much the Footes reassured each other that they'd be back soon, no one knew.

Mr. Foote turned to Daniel. "Likely the Committee will be going to your house, Daniel," he said. "If they haven't already been there."

Daniel looked at his squashed hat. He started for the door, then he came back. He grabbed Beckett's hand, told him he'd see him in the morning, and he rushed away. More than anything else, he wanted to be home when the Committee came. Of course, he wouldn't go to Halifax, feeling the way he did. He'd stay behind like Miss Emily, but he wanted to be with his father when he refused to sign the paper. He wanted to be standing, straight, unflinching, like Beckett, when his father's eyes sought his.

The crowd was already at the head of Daniel's street but by cutting through backyards and jumping fences, Daniel was able to get to his house first. He flung himself into the kitchen. "Have they been here yet?" he cried.

There was no need for anyone to answer; the knock was sounding at the front door. Out on the street the crowd was warming up again. "Tar and feathers! Hell or Halifax!" they cried. "Down with Tories! Down with Leonard's allies!"

It was like having a bad dream twice, Daniel thought, waking up from it, then going back to sleep and having it return worse than ever. The Committee members came into the parlor just as they had at the Footes, they spoke their piece, they put the sheet of white paper down on Mrs. West's black walnut table. Daniel braced himself and waited for his father to look at him. But Dr. West glanced neither at the paper nor at Daniel. He went over the desk and slowly he let down the lid. He took out a pen and a pen wiper and carefully, meticulously, he began wiping the old ink off the pen, polishing it and polishing it, as if it were a piece of silver.

Mrs. West was smiling at the Committee members. "Why, of course, Dr. West will be glad to sign," she said. "As you say, the situation has changed. And a doctor's heart is always with the people."

185

There was no place Daniel could look without shame—not at his mother's clock where the little girl was still waving at him, not at the Committee members, not at Hannah and Sarah, who stood in the doorway. He studied his feet and listened to the scratching of his father's pen. Once his father stopped and Daniel held his breath, thinking his father might have reconsidered, but he was apparently only dipping his pen; the scratching resumed. Daniel pictured the big W in the name *West* and the little letters crowding under its shadow, but he didn't look up even when the men left the house, stopping in the doorway, evidently, to hold the paper aloft for the crowd to see because there was a sudden roar outside, the kind of roar a hunting crowd emits when it has cornered its fox.

Dr. and Mrs. West had come back from the front door. "Rabble!" Mrs. West fanned her face with her handkerchief. "Filthy rabble—all of them." She sighed. "Still, there was nothing else we could do."

Slowly Daniel looked up. "If you're still loyal, you could have owned up to it. You could have gone to Halifax," he said. "The Footes are."

"To what purpose? And what would we do in Halifax?" Mrs. West was closing up the desk. "Likely they'll leave us in peace now."

Daniel was breathing heavily. The whole room had gone unsteady and the beams were bars over his head that threatened to come down. "Peace!" He spit out the word. He couldn't talk to his stepmother. He couldn't look at her any longer. He turned to his father, who was sitting on the couch. "Well?" he shouted. "Well? All my life you've taught me to tell the truth! Yet you sign your name to a lie!"

Dr. West was leaning forward, his head between his hands. A shudder seemed to run through his body but he didn't look up. "I can't go to Halifax, Daniel," he said. "I've made all the fresh starts I can make this year."

"You'd *lie* to keep from going. But you'd send me to England. Oh yes, you're quick enough to send me away."

"You're *young*." Dr. West said the word as if it were life itself and he had relinquished it.

"And it's only in youth, I suppose, that you tell the truth."

Dr. West looked up. His face was drawn and gray with fatigue. "You *must* go to England," he said quietly. "You see what they can do to you."

"And it makes no difference to you how I feel? No difference that I'm no longer a Tory?"

"You'll get over that." Dr. West shook his head as though he was trying to clear his vision. "You're just a boy and you can make a fresh start."

"I'll make a fresh start all right!" Daniel cried. He rushed to the front door. "I'll make my fresh start right here. And now." He looked back at the family. They were all strangers to him. "Away from all of you!" he shouted. "Out of this house!" He hurled himself headlong into the night, slamming the door behind him.

Salem seemed no more familiar to Daniel than his family. It had become a nightmare town in which

187

nothing was real or solid. The houses were suddenly paper houses with trees painted between them. The ground, still muddy from the day's rain, gave under Daniel's feet as he ran, forcing him to run faster lest he find that the ground had no bottom at all. Vaguely Daniel was aware that he was trying to find Jeremy on his rounds but he didn't know where he'd be. Instead Daniel found himself in front of St. Peter's Church but it was only a cardboard church, after all, and the people before it were hollow people dancing about in distorted shadows. Suddenly they made a circle around Daniel.

"Here's Daniel West!" someone shouted. "Tory!"

The chant was taken up by the others. "Tory! Tory!"

Daniel's head was reeling and his mouth was dry "I'm not a Tory," he said.

"Not a Tory!" There was a sudden burst of laughter. Wild laughter mixed with jeers that grew louder and louder. Daniel couldn't see the faces, only the legs lighted up by lanterns on the ground. Legs that danced grotesquely and then suddenly stopped in a circle again.

"You say you're with us?" a voice asked.

Daniel swallowed. "I'm with you."

"Anyone got that letter?"

"Yea. I got it. Don't trust it out of my sight." There was a rattling of paper and a figure stooped over one of the lanterns and began reading. "May it please your Excellency," he said. It was the letter that Daniel and

Beckett had written Governor Hutchison. The letter that Daniel thought his stepmother had thrown away.

"Where did you get that letter?" Daniel started toward the person who was reading but the figures came between. A fist was thrust up in front of his face. And suddenly it was quiet. That terrible quiet when you can hear the world hum. Silently the figures pressed closer until there didn't seem to be air to breathe.

"Peter Ray gave it to us," someone said at last. "Said he stole it from your kitchen." There was a pause. "You don't deny it's yours?"

Daniel was at the peak of the nightmare, at that point when a person begins falling and falling. "I don't deny it." He was panting. Falling and panting. "That was long ago. I've changed since."

"All of a sudden you changed." The quiet broke up into pieces of laughter. "Changed just tonight, did you? Like your father. Scared like your father."

Daniel was falling faster.

"We'll see how you've changed," the voice said. "Shall we give him a chance, boys?"

"Give him a chance."

"All right, Daniel West. You come over to Beckett's house with us right now. You go up and knock at the door. And you speak loud and clear. You say, 'Down with all Tories!' You willing to do that?"

"No!" Daniel's voice whirled into space. "No, I'm not willing. But I'm not a Tory. I'm not a Tory!"

"What are you then?"

Someone in the circle suddenly picked up a rock and flung it at a window of St. Peter's Church. Now everyone had rocks. They were all throwing. The group opened up and a rock was pressed into Daniel's hand.

"What are you then, Daniel West?" a voice shouted in Daniel's ear. "Name it. What are you?"

"I'm a—" Daniel was rolling over and over in the air. He was about to hit ground. Any minute he would crash and be nothing, nothing at all. He lifted his arm and before he knew what he was doing, he had flung the rock at the church window.

He dropped his arm. It wasn't a cardboard church any longer. The rock made a shattering sound as it broke the glass and it was his own church he had desecrated and the figures had faces now. Sam White was hurling a rock. Edward Pine was behind him. Ding-Dong Allison stood at the edge of the group and, stepping out of the shadows, there was Peter Ray with a sneer on his face.

Daniel lunged at Peter. He beat his fists against Peter, releasing a giant energy he didn't know he had. He hurled Peter to the ground and was turning him over, shell side up, rubbing his face in the mud, when all at once Peter melted away from his grasp. Daniel felt himself being lifted. His hands were locked behind his back. Part of the group was helping Peter to his feet and the others were tearing at Daniel's coat. A light was coming nearer. Ding-Dong Allison had a lantern and he was holding it up for the boy who had Daniel's coat. They were going through the pockets.

"Take his Tory money!" Sam White cried. "We'll show him what liberty means!"

All at once Ding-Dong Allison whistled. "Well, what do you know!" he said. "Here's that note I put in the oak tree. He's a real Tory, all right, boys. A Tory spy. Let him have it."

That was all Daniel heard. He was thrown to the ground. When he came to, the first thing he was aware of was that he was lying in the mud. He looked up and saw the belfry of St. Peter's Church. Still lying flat, he felt around the ground. There was broken glass. There was something made of cloth. His jacket, most likely. There was a tight sensation around his neck but he supposed it was just one of his hurts and there were many. He tried to isolate them—his arms, his legs, his face. Bruised, all of them, certainly. Blood around his nose. A bump on his forehead. But nothing too serious, he decided.

And now there was a lantern coming down the street. Daniel tried to get up. He had got as far as a sitting position when the lantern stopped beside him. It was Benjie. Daniel wanted to explain but his mouth wouldn't open and Benjie didn't look interested anyway. All he was doing was staring at a spot on Daniel's chest.

Daniel put his hand up to his chest and there was a piece of heavy paper attached to a string that went around his neck. He lifted it off. Just one word was printed on the paper, TORY.

"That's no news," Benjie said and he walked off down the street, his lantern swinging at his side.

Daniel dropped the paper in the mud and worked himself up to his feet. Slowly he made his way to Jeremy's house.

"Just don't ask me anything tonight," Daniel said to Tillie when she opened the door. "Just let me sleep here. And wake me first thing in the morning. I have to see the *Neptune* sail."

Chapter Twelve

IT WAS JEREMY who woke Daniel in the morning.
He leaned down over the makeshift bed of blankets
on the kitchen floor and touched Daniel on the
shoulder.

"It's morning, lad," he said, "or are you too battered
to recognize it?"

Daniel's eyes were swollen but he forced them open. Tillie had insisted that he take care of his hurts the night before and exchange his muddy clothes for one of Jeremy's nightshirts. She'd cleaned up his clothes after he'd gone to sleep and dried them before the fire.

"Your father was here last night," Jeremy said, "after you were asleep. He was worried about you, lad."

The events of the night took hold of Daniel and he closed his eyes.

"Here," Tillie said, leaning down now too. "Take this wet cloth and hold it over your eyes and nose a minute and you'll feel better. Your father will be sorry to see you in this condition."

"He's not going to see me," Daniel said. He put the cloth over his eyes. "I'm not going home, Jeremy. Maybe not ever. I don't know." Rainbows of light danced in his eyes under the wet cloth. "I'm through with politics. I can't be a Tory. And they won't let me be anything else. Maybe I can't be anything. Not with pride. I wanted to take pride in what I was." His face was so stiff that talking was difficult. "You know what I did last night, Jeremy?" he whispered. "I threw a rock at my own church. I broke the south window."

"Well."

Daniel handed the cloth back to Tillie. "I'm going off." He sat up. "After I see Beckett."

Tillie had a cup of warm milk and some bread ready for him. "Come back afterwards, Daniel," she said. "There's no time to talk now."

Jeremy helped Daniel into his clothes. "Don't do

194

anything hasty, lad," he said. "Doesn't look to me that you're in a condition to be hasty."

Indeed, every movement that Daniel made was in slow motion, but although he ached all over, he felt no pain in any specific part of his body. It was as if his mind was too taken up with its own hurts to feel sorry for an arm or a leg or a badgered nose. Still, as Daniel went toward the dock, his body loosened up somewhat and his mind fastened on the big hurt paramount at the moment. Beckett was leaving.

Normally at a sailing there was a large crowd of people at the waterfront but today people went about their business, ashamed, Daniel thought, turning their backs on the families that were being driven off. Daniel had already learned from Jeremy that there would not be many families leaving. The Whigs had called on only a half dozen Tories, hoping that the others would see the way the wind was blowing and act accordingly. As it turned out, even the governor had been impressed by the violence of the night. He was reported to have given up the idea of putting anyone on the *Scarborough*. Salem would have to wait for its day of reckoning, he said, but he had no doubt that the reckoning would come.

It was a lonely group on the dock, gray figures in a gray morning with a gray sea behind them. Beckett was at the edge of the group and he stepped forward as Daniel approached. He took one look at Daniel's face and frowned.

"You all right?" he asked.

195

Daniel nodded.

"I thought I was the enemy around here. Not you."

"I'm everybody's enemy." Daniel watched a sea gull light on the *Neptune*'s mast. It drew its wings until it had lost its freedom-look and was only an awkward ducklike creature.

"Well, you take care of yourself. I'll likely be back soon. We'll go to the Miseries yet."

Daniel tried to smile but he didn't feel that his smile came out right under his swollen nose.

"Daniel."

"Yes?"

"My father and I have a favor to ask of you."

"I'm glad." Daniel made another attempt at smiling. "I was hoping you'd ask me to do something. It would ease my feelings."

"It's the boat." Beckett pointed into the harbor, where the *Allegiance* bobbed at anchor. "Will you take care of it? Most important, we want you to use it. As if it were your own."

"You call that a favor?"

"It's important to us." Beckett looked down at the dock. "The truth is, and you know it, Daniel," he said slowly, "no one knows when we'll be back. We want to think of our boat sailing around Salem waters. Her sails full."

Daniel couldn't smile now. There was something going on in his throat that made his whole face difficult to manage.

"And something else, Daniel," Beckett said. "You

can't sail a boat in any kind of safety around here with the name *Allegiance* on it. We want you to change the name. Call it anything that would be appropriate to your sentiments."

"I can't do that."

"It's what we want. The boat is yours in every way until we return. You're to think of it as *yours*."

"I can't change its name."

Beckett looked over Daniel's head at the town of Salem. "Call it the *Libera*," he said. "It has a free ring to it that will satisfy the Whigs. And for us, Daniel, our best times have started with that cry."

Daniel swallowed. "All right," he said. "All right."

"And if anything should happen, if you have to leave town with your family—"

"I'm not going anywhere with my family."

"Well, if you should go anywhere, don't worry about it. Just tell Mr. Mansfield. He's promised to help Aunt Emily in our absence."

The Tory families were beginning to walk up the plank to the *Neptune* now. The Footes held back to say good-bye to Daniel and then they went too, Beckett last.

Beckett went to the stern of the schooner and looked out at Salem while the *Neptune* inched away from the dock, then shifted about in the water, the way a racer dances at the starting line. One by one, its sails unfurled. Beckett raised his hand to Daniel but he didn't leave his position. At the end of the dock, Daniel watched the *Neptune* shrink in size. He watched Beckett become smaller and smaller until he was only a dot. Then he was there no longer and after a while the *Neptune* slid over the horizon.

That blasted horizon, Daniel thought angrily. Chopping the world in half. Dividing it in two and then setting one part against the other. Splitting up friendships. Cutting at a person until he didn't know himself any longer.

"I'm not going home," he whispered. "I'm not going back to that Whig-Tory mess. I'm going off." He didn't know what he meant. He didn't know where he'd go but he huddled against the piling and listened to himself talk. "I'm going to get in Beckett's boat," he said, "and I'm going to sail. Off. Alone. Away."

He didn't hear the steps behind him until they were at his elbow and he looked up to see Jeremy. "Knew you wanted to come down here alone to see Beckett," Jeremy said. "But thought you might like company now."

"I'm not fit for company and I'm not going to stay."

Jeremy put his hand on Daniel's arm. "Can't blame you. Not much comfort in the ocean today. You'd be better off at home."

Daniel raised his voice. "That's what I'm saying. I'm not going home. I'm going off."

"What do you mean—off?"

"Off. Away from Salem."

"Where, boy?"

"Anywhere. I'll take Beckett's boat and I'll just go." He didn't want to think where or how. He looked out to sea at all the little islands standing apart, midway to the horizon but holding off from it. Sturdy, independent patches of land, they'd always seemed, defying both the sea and the continent. He thought of Beckett's map with the *x* marking the spot they'd make camp.

"You can't go just anywhere," Jeremy insisted.

Daniel took a deep breath. "I'll go to the Miseries."

"Yes, you can do that. You've camped there before. The weather's good. I reckon a few days—"

Daniel looked at Jeremy as if he didn't understand. "It will be a sight longer than a few days."

"How long?"

"All I know is the going part. I'm not ready to think about the coming back part."

"I don't know what your father will say. I saw him a few minutes ago. Said he was coming down here to see you."

"I've quit listening to what he says." Daniel's face twisted. "He's done nothing but hand me surprises this year. Well, here's one for him."

Jeremy shook his head. "Don't be too hard on your father, lad. He's had a bad year."

"Hard? I'm just not going to think about him." Daniel pushed his hands into his pockets. "I'm going to the Footes' and get the paddles and the sailing gear."

Daniel and Jeremy hadn't reached the end of the dock, however, before they met Dr. West coming their way. When he first looked at Daniel, it was not as a father but as a doctor, sizing up the extent of the injuries.

Daniel turned his face away. "I'll be all right," he said shortly. "I'll take care of myself." A fresh wave of weariness swept over him. He had to get away quickly. He couldn't argue. Or give reasons. Or say what he was. Or think about the night before. Or look at the days ahead. "I'm going to the Miseries," he said. "I'm going to cut loose from all this, here." He waved his hand toward Salem. "And no one's going to stop me."

When he had finished, the two men looked over his head as if he were a patient in bed and they were consulting on the best way to handle him.

"I think maybe he needs to be alone a spell," Dr. West said quietly as if he were issuing a prescription. "He's banged up but it doesn't look serious." He put his hand out and felt Daniel's nose. "Nothing broken."

They talked as if he weren't there. They began to plan about the clothing and supplies he should take with him and Jeremy volunteered to get the necessary things together while Daniel went to the Footes'.

Dr. West turned back to Daniel. "If you have to do this," he said, "it's fortunate you have time. It's some weeks before the *Quero* sails. October ninth is the date. Bear it in mind."

Daniel stared at his father, but his father hadn't finished. He'd dropped his professional tone. He was looking out to sea now, talking half to himself, almost as if he were back in the parlor, taking up the conversation of the night before. "You think I can't understand what you're doing, Daniel," he said slowly. "But I can understand. Wanting to pull up stakes. I can understand."

Daniel winced. He couldn't bear the word *understand* again.

"I can understand." Dr. West sighed. "We're cut from the same piece of cloth, you and I, Daniel. We like peace."

How could a person speak across such depths of misunderstanding? "We're not alike at all," Daniel said and turned to go to the Footes'.

When he got back, he worked grimly at getting ready. In addition to picking up the sailing equipment, he had brought back a brush and some lampblack, and before doing anything else, he pulled the skiff close to the sloop. Standing up, he blacked out the *Allegiance* and above it he printed *Libera*. The letters weren't as steady as they would have been if he'd had the boat on dry land but they were clear enough and they made the boat, for the time being, his own. Jeremy, meanwhile, was organizing the practical necessities—the clothing and food he'd collected at the Wests' house before Dr. West had left on his round of sick calls. Daniel pulled up the anchor, paddled the sloop to the dock, and began loading.

But when it was all done, Jeremy insisted that Daniel postpone his departure until afternoon, after he'd had a full meal. Even then, he wouldn't let Daniel go until he'd checked every item he could think of.

"Ax?" Jeremy asked from the dock.

"In the case there." Daniel was in the boat and pointed under the bow at Beckett's tool case.

"Fishing pole?"

Daniel nodded.

"Frying pan. Cooking pot. Water jug. Blankets." Jeremy reached the end of his list. "You have provisions for about a week. But you'll likely be ready to come home before that."

"We'll see."

"Well, I'll be coming out to visit you in any case. And I'll bring fresh supplies."

"All right. And thanks for everything."

"Just one thing, boy—" Jeremy hesitated. "What are you going to do by yourself all day, every day?"

"Count the daisies." Daniel managed the first real grin of the day, and cast off.

Daniel had never managed the boat alone but it was as if the boat understood, even his weariness. He headed it into the wind, hoisted the two sails, one after the other, and took the tiller. "There we are, mate," he sighed. "Clear sailing." The boat dipped its bow into the waves and took off, out of the harbor, past Winter Island, making the wide arc between the Neck and that knob of land known as Great Haste, and finally to open sea.

It was five miles from Salem Harbor to the Miseries and with each mile Daniel and the boat reached a deeper understanding. The boat, its sails filled with an easterly wind, shielded Daniel from a full view of the mainland so that as they approached the Miseries, the

202

islands looked more remote than they were, a land unto itself, in its original state, unaware of people and their cross-purposes.

"That's right, mate," Daniel whispered. "Around the island. Into that cove there."

The boat nosed into the cove. The sails flapped for a minute as the boat came about; then Daniel lowered the sails and dropped anchor and the boat hesitated and settled down in the water.

Daniel sat on the bow. "Now we're here," he said, "and there's no hurry to do anything. No one to ask us questions. No sides to take. No thinking to do. We can just look. As long as we want to."

It was a silent place. Daniel sat still getting accustomed to the silence. With Beckett along, he had never realized how silent rocks and trees were, how indifferent they were to a person's presence. He was almost averse to going ashore. It was as if he'd be intruding on creation itself, dragging history into a place that was free of time, dumping his concerns into a well of silence. Daniel shivered. Maybe it was that silence, he thought, that had got man going in the first place, way back at the beginning. Maybe he'd moved rocks about and swung his ax, just trying to make nature take notice. There was an abandoned house on the island, erected a century before by a Captain Curwen, but the house, gray and weathered, its roof sagging at one end, grasses growing up the steps, had assumed the same character as the rocks and the trees. If it remembered people at all, it was only as mistakes.

"Wish you could go ashore with me, mate," Daniel whispered. He was overwhelmingly tired. He pulled up the skiff which was tied to the back of the boat, loaded his supplies into it, untied the line, and rowed to shore. He'd make a more permanent settlement another day; all he'd do now was to unload. When he'd finished, Daniel wrapped himself in a blanket and lay down beyond the tide line. In full daylight and in sight of the boat, he fell asleep.

The next day Daniel put his supplies on the porch of the old house, a ready-made cover against the rain. He filled his jug with water from the fresh pond, gathered twigs and driftwood and built a fire on the beach. Beside this he made himself a bed of crossed limbs and grass and leaves so that in fair weather he could sleep on the beach in sight of the boat. He found an old plank washed up on the shore and he took it near the fire, set it up on two stones and placed his cooking and eating utensils on it. He glanced at the *Libera*. "Now we've got a shelf and a fire and bed," he said. "We're fixed to stay a long time."

He looked back at the island. At the trees and the rocks. There was one particular tree that was even more aloof than the others. It was a tall pine. It shot straight up from the ground, stiff and haughty, and didn't even bother to branch out until three-fourths of the way to the top. Stationed at the edge of the beach, it had a superior air as if it knew it could outlast anything. Daniel stepped toward the tree. "We're fixed to stay a long time," he repeated.

As the days went by, Daniel discovered that one of the main troubles with being alone on an island was that a person never felt the right size. He was always either too small or too big. In the daytime when he walked about the island, he felt enormous, awkward, bungling. His footsteps, no matter how quietly he tried to walk, crashed through the undergrowth, triggering off a chain of frightened responses—the warning cry of an osprey; the sudden beat of wings as quail, flushed from their hiding places, rose, startled, in the air; the rustle of leaves as rabbits scurried for cover. Even when he was sitting down, he felt huge. The gulls looked at him with bloodshot eyes and veered away.

At night it was different. Wrapped in his blankets on his beach bed, staring at the sea stretched around him and stars spread above him, Daniel cringed at his smallness. There were so many stars. Night after night he watched shooting stars drop out of the sky, but after they'd fallen, he searched the sky but he could never tell where they'd been. Sometimes he felt so small, he wondered if he was there at all and then he'd talk to the *Libera* anchored in the cove before him. "We're just used to people, you and I," he'd say. "It takes time to feel settled." And he'd tell the *Libera* what he'd done that day. "Caught two flounder," he'd say. Or "Got myself a mess of clams." Or "Gathered firewood today."

The one spot Daniel avoided was High Point, the only place from which a person could see Salem. Once on a particularly clear day when he and Beckett had climbed High Point they had been able to pick out individual landmarks—Winter Island, the Neck, the tower of St. Peter's Church. They'd seen the tower clearly. And if there was one thing Daniel did not want to see now, it was St. Peter's Church. If there was one thing he didn't want to think about, it was that broken south window. He'd rather look at that haughty pine tree any day.

At the end of the first week Jeremy came with fresh supplies. He didn't unload right away, however, because he was sure Daniel would be ready to go back.

"I'm not going back," Daniel insisted. "I like it here. I'm getting along fine." He scuffed at stones at the water's edge. "I'll stay until there's no more talk about the *Quero*. If need be, I'll stay until the *Quero* sails."

Jeremy didn't look as if he believed Daniel. He came out every week, always expecting Daniel to go back, always surprised when he wouldn't. "Your father says not to argue," he'd say. "He says he understands. You'll come around." There was only once that Jeremy went further. "I'd have thought you'd have come around before this," he said. "Or else have gone in and brought your father around. He's not likely to pick you up bodily, boy, and put you on the *Quero*."

"I've told them I'm not a Tory," Daniel said stubbornly. "And they won't believe me. I'm not going to keep saying what I am and saying what I am. Over and over."

Jeremy didn't bring up the subject again. He'd take out his fishing pole that he'd brought along and they'd stand on the rocks and throw out their lines together. Sometimes he brought a pail and he'd pick a mess of blueberries to take home to Tillie. While Jeremy was there, Daniel hardly noticed the circling ospreys or the sound of his own footsteps. For a few hours it seemed that he and Jeremy were on an excursion and in a short time they'd be taking their fish back for Tillie to fry. But after Jeremy's first visit, Daniel knew the island was only waiting. Once Jeremy had gone, that pine tree would seem prouder and more standoffish than ever. Sometimes Daniel would go over to the tree and strike it with his fist. "You think I have to grow roots to get along here?" he'd cry.

Jeremy brought news to the island as well as supplies. Tillie had a pet goose that she'd named Adams, after Samuel. Benjie had quit school and was working for Mr. Derby. There was other news too. While the sumac turned red on the Miseries and the wild geese flew south, General Gage and the people of Massachusetts were coming closer and closer to war. The thunder was rolling, Jeremy said, and there was no telling when it would break into a storm. In the county of Suffolk a document had been drawn up and adopted by the Continental Congress which specifically defied the authority of Parliament. All over the province people were arming, gathering weapons and artillery and

hiding them against a day when they'd be needed.
General Gage had his troops, including the regiment
from Winter Island, concentrated in Boston now where
they could be moved anywhere he thought arming was
taking place. He'd already marched against Charlestown and seized 250 barrels of powder which the
citizenry had hidden. It was only because he'd done
it so quickly that there hadn't been a conflict. The
whole countryside had been in arms by morning but
by that time the British troops had left. And if the
province was collecting arms, Jeremy said, a person
could be sure of one thing. Salem wouldn't lag behind.
Nor would General Gage spare any pains to bring
Salem to its knees. If not in one way, in another. He
was likely making plans right now, Jeremy said. The
General Court was scheduled to meet in Salem again
on October fifth.

Daniel had drawn a calendar in the hard sand at
the top of the beach. He'd marked it out in squares
for each day with a stick and put a stone in each of
the squares. At the end of the day he picked up that
stone and threw it into the sea, listening to the dull
plop as it fell into the water and watching the rippled
circles widen and disappear. The last day on his
calendar was October ninth.

Gradually the stones became fewer, the nights colder,
the sumac redder, browning in spots, until there were
only five stones left in his calendar. It was a Friday,
the day that Jeremy normally made his visits, and it
was also the day the General Court was to meet in

Salem. Daniel had been keeping an eye out for Jeremy all morning but when a boat finally did round the bend into the cove, Daniel was at the fresh pond, preparing to fill his water jug. The pond was afloat with yellow leaves and he had to push them away to fill the jug. He was on his knees, his arm extended over the water, when he noticed the boat. But it wasn't Jeremy's boat. It was a small boat, like Jeremy's, which could be beached, but it wasn't Jeremy standing by the mast, lowering the sail. It was a shorter person—slight and wiry, a boy. He sat down, reached for the oars but before lowering them into the water, he looked at the island and called out.

"Ahoy there, Daniel!"

Daniel found his arm trembling, the jug still suspended from it.

"Daniel West! Are you there, Daniel?"

It was Charlie Putnam. He put the oars into the water and rowed to shore, pulling the boat up after him. He lifted out a box, carried it to the fire, and then he sat down. He was going to stay.

Slowly Daniel set the jug on the ground and as he stood up, Charlie, alert to the noise, stood too.

"Wondered where you were," Charlie called.

Daniel walked down to the beach but although Charlie tossed him sentences, Daniel made no return. He didn't speak until he had reached the fire. "You're the last person I expected to pay me a visit, Charlie Putnam." Sometimes after a week alone, his voice, in normal conversation, sounded stiff and unused. "But maybe it's not a visit." He nodded at the box. "Maybe it's just a delivery."

"Jeremy sent me with your supplies. He couldn't come today. He wanted to be around for the Court meeting."

"Much obliged."

But Charlie wasn't ready to go. He scuffed at the ashes around the fire. "I wanted to come anyway. You've been on my mind, Daniel. Beckett leaving and you running off right afterward. Holing up here."

Daniel turned his back and looked at the pond, still except for an almost imperceptible dreamlike swirl that carried the fallen leaves around and around. "Didn't suppose you'd care to speak to someone who's supposed to be a Tory."

He didn't turn around. He kept his back to Charlie even when Charlie spoke.

"Jeremy says you're no longer a Tory. He says you've changed."

"And I suppose, like all the rest, you and Benjie think I changed when my father did. Because I was scared."

There was no answer.

"It's what you and Benjie think, isn't it?"

"Well, you know Benjie." Charlie sighed. "Words don't mean a thing to him. Only deeds. And he says if you're really a Whig, you'll prove it, one way or another. He says there'll be ample opportunity. You don't know what things are like in town now, Daniel."

"What are they like?"

"Like a tinderbox. Everyone's jumpy. As if there

210

were going to be an explosion and anything could set it off. Maybe the General Court will. Maybe even today. The Whigs have defied the governor again."

Slowly Daniel turned around. "What do you mean —defied?"

Charlie explained that in accordance with the king's wishes, the governor had selected the councilors to the Court instead of providing for an election and, as might be expected, the people were resisting. They had threatened the governor's councilors and demonstrated so violently against them that the governor was afraid for their lives if they were to travel from Boston to Salem. So he'd called off the Court session altogether but the Whig representatives were paying no attention to the order. They were meeting in Salem anyway as if the session hadn't been canceled. It was said they were going to form themselves into a provincial congress and go ahead with governing as though the governor didn't exist.

"So you see," Charlie said, "you can't blame folks for being jumpy. You can't blame Benjie for thinking a person who stays off by himself values peace more than showing his colors." He lowered his voice. "Or else he's just scared."

Daniel walked over to the box of supplies and began unloading it, taking one thing out after another so quickly he had no idea what he was handling. Everyone, he thought bitterly, believed they knew him so well. They thought they could see deep inside him where the reasons were and then name them off, one, two, three.

"Just what good do you suppose either you or I could do for Salem," he asked, "at our age?"

Charlie shrugged. "Maybe none. But a person would never be sure unless he were there." He reached into his pocket. "I've got something else for you, Daniel. A letter from your father Jeremy asked me to give you." He handed over the letter. "You know your father hasn't been well, do you?"

Daniel put the letter in his pocket. "No. I didn't know."

"He's bothered with his gout again. Not as bad as that last spell in June, Jeremy says, but sometimes he has to resort to crutches." Charlie was fingering his hat. "Well, if there's nothing I can do, Daniel, I guess I'll go back and see what's going on."

"Thanks for coming."

Charlie still hesitated. "No messages you'd like me to relay? You want to read that letter before I go? Maybe you'll change your mind."

"Maybe."

Daniel took the letter out of his pocket. He sat down on the sand and opened it. At the sight of the familiar handwriting, he pictured his father opening the lid of his desk and taking out the pen he'd used to sign the Whigs' paper.

Dear Daniel, the letter said, *I have every confidence you'll be home within the next two days. As you know, the* Quero *sails October ninth. I pray you will not make it necessary for me to come out and persuade you, but if you have not returned by the seventh, no matter what*

*my physical condition, I shall get a boat and come out.
If by this time, you do not know what is in your best
interest, I shall ask you to trust me, as hard as that
may seem."*

Daniel folded the letter slowly. "No," he said. "No
messages."

"If it's only a matter of differences with your father,"
Charlie said, "seems to me you could brave them out
on shore as well as here." He started for the boat.
"You're sure you won't come back with me? Find out
what's going on at Court?"

"No. I won't go back."

Charlie shook his head. "Maybe Benjie is right. He
says whatever you are, you're only lukewarm." He
climbed into his boat.

Daniel watched Charlie sail around the cove. As
soon as he was out of sight, Daniel began packing his
belongings. He looked at the *Libera*.

"We're not going back there, mate," he said. "Tomorrow morning we're going up the coast. I don't
know where. We're just going where he can't find us."

He went up to the porch of the old house, packed
up the things he had there and brought them to the
beach. He started up to the pond for the water jug
he'd left when Charlie came. He had to go past the
pine tree but he didn't look at it until he was right
beside it and an osprey startled him into looking. It
rose, screaming, from the topmost branches and then
Daniel looked. At the angry osprey. At the green crown
of branches so far up that stiff trunk that not even the

wind could bow them. All it could do was to shake the branches slowly. Daniel had watched the wind at work in it. He knew. The tree never lost its composure. Suddenly Daniel threw himself at the trunk of the tree. He kicked it. He beat his hands on the bark. "You think you're lord of the island!" he cried.

Chapter Thirteen

DANIEL COULDN'T SLEEP that night. Not because of the stars. Nor because he was planning to leave early in the morning. He just couldn't get Charlie's words out of his mind. He kept thinking of Salem like a tinderbox in the night with the General Court fulminating at its center. Lying on the beach, wrapped in his blankets, he stared at the moon, so steady and cold and white, and under it the island and the sea so still and peaceful, it was hard to imagine that a few miles away under the same moon people had got themselves in such a tangle, there seemed no way for them to get out. What did the moon see, he wondered, from its high vantage point? Right now looking down on Salem, what did the moon see?

Daniel pictured Salem, its taverns full, Samuel Adams likely walking even at this time of night, Jeremy on his rounds, perhaps even now on Derby Wharf calling out the hour. He looked at the moon for confirmation but the moon would confirm nothing. He thought of Ding-Dong Allison's shack at the edge of the Common; he thought of the regiment lined up the length of King Street. He thought of St. Peter's Church and the moon streaming in that broken window. He rolled over on his stomach and tried to turn his mind into blackness but the moon was too bright. He imagined he could feel the moonlight playing on his back, on the beach, on the rocks and trees. On High Point. It was from there, and there only, that a person could get a moon's-eye view of the world.

Daniel sat up. He glanced toward the *Libera* standing at attention in the cove. "Likely a person couldn't see anything from High Point," he said. He slipped on his jacket. "Likely he couldn't even make out the Neck." He put on his boots. "Nothing to see anyway," he said. "A town asleep." He stood up. "I'll be back in a few minutes," he said and he set off up the beach, under the pine tree, taking the path that led straight to High Point.

It wasn't so very high, he noted, and the moonlight was, after all, only a soft glow. He hadn't reached the top, however, when he broke into a run. The sky over Salem was a rosy red. The red began at the bottom and went up, fading as it went. The band of red at the bottom was bright. At first he didn't realize what it meant. He'd never seen the sky so red before. It must be the color of war, he thought, and then it came to him what it was. Salem, or part of Salem, was on fire.

Daniel didn't remember getting back to the beach. When he first became aware of what he was doing, he was fumbling with the line that tied the skiff to its stake on the shore. Indeed, the night seemed to be strung with lines that had to be adjusted. The skiff had to be made fast to the stern of the *Libera*, the anchor raised, the halyards pulled, the mainsheet trimmed. His hand on the tiller, he leaned forward, as a rider leans to give his horse its head, encouraging the *Libera*, impressing it with the need for speed.

Long before he reached the harbor, he smelled the smoke and saw billows rising from the town. As he came nearer, he was able to narrow down the location. The fire was not at the waterfront, not near the Common; the smoke came from the west, from Daniel's own side of town. He headed west for the dock at Ingalls Cove, adjusted the lines again, and ran.

At the waterfront he was intercepted by a woman who thrust a bucket into his hand.

"Town House Square," she cried. "It's at Town House Square."

"Was there fighting?"

The woman looked uncomprehending.

"Was the fire set?" Daniel asked desperately.

"Who knows if it was set? It's going." The woman started to push at Daniel; then she peered into his face. "You're Dr. West's boy, aren't you?" she asked. "It's your street, boy. Your house is gone. Dr. Whittaker's meetinghouse. Peter Frye's. The whole street."

His bucket at his side, Daniel pressed through crowds of women and children who waited for news at a safe distance. He found himself at the Town House beside double lines of men that fanned out in all directions—down King Street, up toward the Witches' Well, across to the river on one side, over to the harbor on the other. Buckets of water were passed up one line and empty buckets went from hand to hand down the other. The three hand fire engines were stationed at three corners of the street before the Town House in an effort to save the rest of Salem and keep the fire from spreading. Ladders leaned against every house and men clung to the roofs, wetting them down, fighting sparks.

A fire warden, distinguished by the five-foot pole he carried, shouted at Daniel to go back down the street and once there he was pushed into a bucket line and became part of the rhythmical movement to which the whole town swayed. Facing sideways, his feet planted far apart, he swung to the right to receive an empty bucket, then swung to the left to pass it on. To the right and then to the left. He didn't move easily. All the time his eyes were searching the line of men for his father; he was like a pendulum in need of oil, jerking back and forth. It was a while before Daniel realized that not only was his father not in his line, there was no one near him he recognized.

"You men from Marblehead in this line?" he asked as he passed a bucket to his left.

"Some of us. There are well over a hundred of us, all told."

Daniel swayed back in the other direction. "Where did it start?"

"Peter Frye's warehouse."

Back to the left. "Was it set?"

"Most likely."

To the right. "Was it a Whig after Peter Frye?"

"Wouldn't be surprised. Frye said he wouldn't interfere with the government. But he kept talking. Tory talk. Especially the last few days with the Court preparing to convene."

Daniel broke the rhythm to ask the next question. "Anyone hurt?"

The answer came from the right. "One old lady. A Mrs. Fields. And they caught some boys looting. Name of White and Pine, I understand."

Daniel rocked back to his other neighbor. He had to force himself to the automatic movement. Sometimes he had to be nudged. Sometimes it was all he could do to stay in the line at all. It was *his* house that was burning, he told himself. *His* father that had been pushed into the streets. And it was a Whig who had apparently done it. Someone on *his* side that had endangered the whole town. Right and left, right and left, he shifted his weight from one foot to another.

The sky had lightened to morning before the signal came that the fire was under control and the lines could break up. The fire wardens shouted that buckets could be reclaimed later in the day at the Common. And all Marbleheaders, he called out, were invited to Webb's Tavern for a free breakfast at Salem's expense.

Members of the three Salem fire clubs stayed on guard around the smoldering ruins. Eight houses, fourteen shops, and Mr. Whittaker's church were gone and only the blackened frame of the saddlemaker's shop stood up in the ruins. The rest was a smoking mass of rubbish with here and there a recognizable object that had survived—an andiron, a charred table, a pot, a kettle, a washtub. Men who had worked at some distance from the fire stood quietly now surveying the destruction. As Daniel came up, they stepped aside for him to pass.

Daniel walked down School Street to where his house had stood. All that remained was the pump in the backyard and standing beside it was his father. He was leaning on his crutches, looking not at the site of the house but at the site of the barn. Daniel put his arm around his father's shoulder and felt it tremble at the touch. For a while neither of them spoke as they contemplated the pile of ashes.

"It was in the west corner of the barn," Dr. West finally whispered, "that her things were." Tears were running down his face. "Mind how we set her things up in that west corner? Her bed, her dishes, her candle table?"

Daniel nodded.

"Gone. Everything gone."

Daniel tightened his arm.

"We saved the horse. But the rest—everything in the barn—it went." Dr. West took a long shuddering breath. "But you're here now, Daniel. I knew you'd come back. I couldn't have gone through this looking without you."

Daniel took hold of the pump handle and without being aware of what he was doing, gave it a push or two. The pump coughed and then let out a stream of water. "Is Jonathon all right?" he asked. "And Sarah?"

"Yes. They are at the Footes' house. Miss Emily has asked us to stay with her as long as we want."

"Did you save anything in the house?"

"My doctor's satchel, that's all. The clothes are gone, the furniture, my books, my medicines. Everything." Dr. West leaned forward on his crutches, his face so drawn, so old and tired-looking that Daniel felt his anger rising again, at the Whigs, at the Liberty Boys, at whoever it was who had started the fire.

"Signing those papers—it wasn't enough, was it, Daniel?" Dr. West sighed. "Peter Frye signed and still they wouldn't leave him alone." He shook his head. "There's no peace to be found in this country. No way to be safe." Shifting about on his crutches, with

221

his house reduced to ashes around him, he looked, Daniel thought, not as if he were part of a country preparing for war but as if he were a victim of a country that had already been devastated by one. He didn't say anything about the *Quero* or about future plans. He just clumped down the middle of the smoky street toward the Footes' with Daniel at his side.

Salem went to bed at dawn that day and slept through the morning. The ashes smoldered at Town House Square; the empty fire buckets stood lined up at the Common waiting to be reclaimed. The two boys who had been caught looting at the scene of the fire, Samuel White and Edward Pine, slept in the jail, waiting for the punishment that would be meted out to them later in the day. Even Jeremy slept. He had stayed at the fire longer than anyone else, wandering around the streets, re-creating the disaster in his mind, trying to think how he could have prevented it, but he'd been on the other side of town when the fire broke out and the wind had been blowing the wrong way for him to smell it. "I told them," he'd say. "I told them they needed more night watchmen." Over and over he went over the details, and at last he too went home to bed.

The only people stirring in the early morning were the members of the General Court. They met in the scorched Town House, resolved themselves into a provincial congress and then quickly adjourned to more comfortable quarters in Concord.

They had already gone by the time Salem awoke, hardly able to believe that the events of the night had not been a great community nightmare. One by one people drifted to Town House Square to see the devastation, to discuss it, and look around for someone to blame. Rumors started and died and started again, Tories blamed Whigs and Whigs, angry at being blamed, turned against Tories harder than ever. Some people were even preparing to leave town altogether.

There was no way to prove anything and no one to punish except the two boys waiting in jail. Three o'clock was the time set for Samuel White and Edward Pine to be tied to the public whipping post. It was theft they were to be punished for, but they'd been on the scene of the fire so soon after the outbreak, many people held them responsible for more.

At quarter to three Daniel was on the way to the Common to pick up the two fire buckets that belonged to the Wests and the Footes. Dr. West was in bed, his leg having taken a turn for the worse. The rest of the family was in a daze, stricken by the enormity of their losses. Every once in a while Mrs. West's eyes would go blank and then as if she were surfacing after a dive, she would come up with another item to be added to the inventory of things that had gone. It was only when Daniel was at the edge of the crowd at the jail that he felt himself emerging from the shock of what had happened.

Charlie Putnam was in the crowd. "See you came back, after all," he said, moving to Daniel's side.

223

"Yes, I came back."

"I'm sorry about your house. I told you things were bad here. And they'll be worse before they're better. You going to stay and see it out?"

It was as if he'd never left, Daniel thought. He watched the jail door open. The jailkeeper came out with Samuel White and Edward Pine behind him. They had such a sly, hangdog look about them that Daniel felt his anger turning over inside him again. It was as if they knew more than they were telling and were sorry only that they'd been caught.

"Life is going to be hard around here," Charlie said, "for people who don't like contention."

Daniel set his mouth grimly. "I don't suppose anyone likes it."

"But there are those who face up to it." (Samuel White shuffled over to the whipping post.) "And those," Charlie said, "who run off." (The jailkeeper ordered Samuel to raise his arms.) "To the Miseries. That's where some of them go."

The jailkeeper was tying Samuel White's hands to the top of the post. "Yes, and there are *those*," Daniel said angrily, pointing at Samuel White. "Who get us into trouble. Who burn down houses. They're on *your* side."

"On your side too, I supposed," Charlie said quietly, "from what you said. Or have you changed again?"

Daniel spun around to face Charlie. "It's easy enough for you," he said. "It wasn't your house that was burned to the ground."

The crowd was roaring now as the jailkeeper raised

his whip. "For stealing goods," he cried. "Samuel White. Fifteen stripes."

"Make that whip sing!" someone cried.

"He set the fire!"

"Drive him out of town!"

Daniel turned and pushed his way out of the crowd, heading toward the Common where the buckets were. The voice of the jailkeeper followed him. He was calling out the number of stripes as he gave them.

"One!" he cried as Daniel passed Webb's Tavern.

"Two!" Daniel turned into Epes's Lane.

"Three!" He was approaching St. Peter's Church.

"Four!" Daniel was in front of the church. He stopped and looked up. There was the south window with a large hole in the center. A jagged hole. All around the edge of the hole sharp pieces of glass pointed to the place the rock had gone through. Daniel found himself shivering.

"For all my talk," he whispered, "I'm no better than Sam White." He remembered the night he'd been so angry to find slops on the steps of the church, but that hole in the window was his own doing.

"Eight," the jailkeeper shouted. "Nine."

And then he'd run away. It was true. He'd run away, seeking peace like his father.

"Ten. Eleven."

Daniel closed his eyes as if the whip were being applied to his own back. He'd raised his colors halfway up the mast. And then he'd thrown a rock.

Samuel White was crying at the whipping post, begging the jailkeeper to leave off.

225

"Thirteen."

Did a person ever know what he'd do until he was pressed and saw himself doing it? Did he know what he was at all?

"Fourteen."

Did any of them know what they were doing? A weak new country pitting itself against a mighty empire. Hiding a few measly barrels of powder here. A cannon or two there. Burning itself down in the process.

"Fifteen."

And all he had to contribute was anger. First against one side. Then against the other. Against himself. He was the weakest link of all.

Daniel stood before St. Peter's Church while another fifteen stripes were laid on the back of Edward Pine. Then he walked to the Common.

Some of the buckets had already been picked up but there were hundreds still left, fanning out in all directions from the flagpole. Whig and Tory buckets together, each with a name or initial painted on the side. Daniel stood still for a moment and simply looked at them. All those buckets put to such hard use, standing now under the flagpole that had over the years witnessed so much—good times and bad times but never a worse time. Certainly there'd never been a worse time for him, yet suddenly he found himself stirred by the sight of those buckets. It was queer that buckets should arouse him, he thought. Just buckets. Yet looking at them, he felt his throat knot. He had to stay in this town, he thought. He had to see what would happen. And when the time came that he was pressed again, he had to see what he'd do.

Daniel walked up and down the lines until he found the two buckets he was looking for and then he went to Miss Emily's.

Chapter Fourteen

DANIEL DIDN'T sail on the *Quero*. There was no trouble about it at all. Dr. West recognized that a boy couldn't start off for England with only the clothes on his back and the few old things he'd had on the island. It would take a while to get their affairs sufficiently in order for them to make any move, he said.

Dr. West was lying in bed at Miss Emily's as they talked. Gaunt and pale, he stared at the unfamiliar room around him. Maybe they'd all go to England, he said. The whole family. In the spring. The first boat out in the spring. Winter was coming on and they wouldn't want to take the trip in rough weather. And he wasn't fit to go now. Maybe they could make it through the winter here. Wars didn't generally start in winter, he said.

Suddenly the sight of the unfamiliar room seemed too much for Dr. West. He closed his eyes and turned toward the wall. "Oh, I don't know what we'll do," he sighed. "I don't know. But I can't spare you just now, Daniel. You should be leaving but I can't spare you."

Daniel leaned down and put his hand on his father's shoulder. "We could build another house," he whispered. "We could stay and see it through together."

It was weeks before Dr. West could get up again and even more weeks before he could venture out. During this time Daniel tried to bring only good news to the house. Salem would likely be free from any organized activity from the Liberty Boys, he said. Daniel had gone to Ding-Dong Allison's shack soon after the fire and found it empty, stripped of everything. Mr. Allison had evidently overstepped himself, and was gone. As for the danger of fire, Daniel told his father that a committee had been formed to help Jeremy with his night watch. Everything Daniel said was designed to reassure his father. One day he went to the site of their house and picking through the ashes, he found the big iron key to the front door. He brought it back and without comment he put it on the bureau of his father's room. His father never mentioned the key but Daniel noticed when it disappeared from the bureau and then he began telling his father about the other people on School Street who were beginning to rebuild their homes. The foundation was going up for Peter Frye's new house, he said; the saddlemaker was getting lumber for a new shop.

Daniel didn't mention news that might cause alarm. Wars didn't begin in winter, his father had said, so Daniel didn't tell him when the people of Portsmouth, New Hampshire, forced the British commander of the fort there to surrender ninety-seven kegs of powder and over a hundred small arms. When word came in December that the king himself acknowledged that only blows could settle the difference with New England, Daniel didn't speak of it. The province was ruling itself these days, paying taxes to men they had appointed and not to the governor's representatives, trying their cases before magistrates of their own selection, not the governor's. The provincial congress had established a committee for procuring arms and had appointed a Salem man, David Mason, as a member. In Boston, Paul Revere, the foremost rider for the Committee of Safety, was watching General Gage's every move, whether it was winter or not. But if Dr. West knew about any of this, it wasn't from Daniel.

It was a mild winter. Mrs. West spent much of her time sewing, replacing the clothes and linens that had been lost in the fire. On fair days Hannah went shell hunting on the Neck. Jonathon began to walk and Sarah started to embroider a sampler. Miss Emily had a book of sampler patterns and Sarah picked out the shortest quotation she could find, "Behold the day cometh." Even so, she said, there were over a thousand cross-stitches when you included the border and the name and date. Every evening she would show Daniel how much she had accomplished. By January she had finished the border, a frame of red and blue stitches, and she had filled in "Behold."

On the surface, life seemed peaceful enough. Mr. Nicholls had left the school and in order not to miss out on studying altogether, Daniel had made arrangements not only to use Captain Pickering's library, which was one of the finest in town, but also to secure the captain's guidance in a program of reading. Every morning Daniel would sit at the desk before the west window of the Pickering parlor between two walls of books, and he would go over the laws of logic, translate Latin and Greek passages, and sometimes solve mathematical problems that Captain Pickering set out for him.

The captain was so busy with affairs of the province, however, that although he made Daniel welcome, he didn't have much time for him. A tall, stern-faced man, he would stride in and out of the room, always fuming, it seemed, about the state of affairs in Salem. All over the province companies of Minute Men were being formed to come to the defense of their communities on a minute's notice. And what about Salem? Captain

Pickering would strike his fist against his leg in exasperation. Salem was doing nothing. The First Essex Regiment had been marking time under the Tory leadership of Colonel Browne, who had refused to quit his post. Finally, the officers of the regiment had resigned in a body, and then what? A person would think, Captain Pickering said, that some effective action would be taken. But no. The regiment was still so disorganized, it might as well not exist. "And if the British should strike here," he'd say, "we're just not ready. Nowhere near ready."

Nor was Daniel ready. Over the winter months he couldn't see that he had progressed in readiness at all. He'd kept himself so busy at Captain Pickering's and at home that not once in all this time had he even declared himself.

Yet, ready or not, Salem was making itself one of the most vulnerable spots in the province. It was common knowledge that the Derbys had donated some iron cannon to Salem and even now they were at Robert Foster's blacksmith shop on the other side of the North River being mounted. And with David Mason on the committee to procure arms, it was only reasonable to assume that if he hadn't already brought artillery into town, he would be doing so.

Sometimes after Captain Pickering had stormed from the room, Daniel would look out the window at the fruit trees which stood on the west side of the Pickering house and think how, deep inside where the sap was, those trees were already getting ready for spring. Then he'd go home and ask his father if he didn't want to draw up plans for a new house but his father always said no, he guessed not. Often after one of his father's noes, Daniel would go over to the North River where the *Libera* was tied up for the winter. He'd climb in and with his hand on the tiller, he'd listen to Mr. Foster pounding on the anvil and he'd wonder how a person or a town or even a country, for that matter, ever felt ready. He'd wonder what any of them would do if pressed. And himself, most of all.

Winter seldom eased off in Salem before the end of March, although sometimes for an isolated day it might quit. People said on those occasions that winter was just letting the warm weather through while it caught its breath, then it would come roaring back harder than ever. There was such a day in February that year. It was cold the day before and undoubtedly it would be cold the day afterward, but the day itself was gentle and warm, a respite, with none of the responsibilities that a true spring day brings—no call to plant or prune or clean or paint—and for those who said wars didn't begin in winter, there was no call even to worry. Besides, it was Sunday.

As soon as breakfast was over, Daniel headed for Jeremy's. It would be a shame, he thought, on such a day to let the *Libera* stand idle and Jeremy agreed. When church was over, they'd go for a sail. Jeremy was not one of those who believed that wars didn't begin in winter but he didn't believe there'd be trouble on a Sunday.

Daniel had brought everything with him—Beckett's tool case, paddles, sails, so that after church all they'd have to do was to rig the sails and take off. He and Jeremy walked down to the dock near the North Bridge where the *Libera* was tied up. Jeremy glanced across the river at Robert Foster's shop. Two weeks ago Colonel Mason had delivered a brass cannon to the store of arms there, but if General Gage knew about it, Jeremy reasoned, he would have taken action before this. Jeremy squatted down to pull the *Libera* close. And if the general were planning anything, he said, Paul Revere would have warned them. No one ever put anything over on Paul Revere. They stowed away the gear and Jeremy grinned. "We'll take our lunch," he said. "I'll get Tillie to make us some and, Daniel, why don't you go to church with us?"

Recently the Wests had been having prayers at home on a Sunday morning. Except for a few of the most stalwart Tories, no one attended St. Peter's Church any more. The broken windows had never been replaced and they weren't going to be. The church was still the prime target for Whig abuse and if there were new windows, they'd only be broken again. Not even the people who attended church escaped abuse. They'd had to build a ledge around the gallery inside so the members of the congregation on the main floor would be protected from the young Whig boys who went to church deliberately to spit on those below. This Sunday, however, instead of attending the short family service, Daniel agreed to go with Tillie and Jeremy to the North Meeting House near the bridge.

With the boat all set, Daniel went home to put on his Sunday clothes, thinking as he walked that Salem had never looked so peaceful. Smoke curled leisurely up from the chimneys; sparrows chirped on gateposts. Big houses and small, shops and barns—they all looked of a piece, as if they got on together. On School Street the rebuilding was almost completed. Only Dr. West's lot was vacant. Dr. West had arranged for the ashes and rubbish to be carted away and Daniel had himself chopped down the burned skeleton of the hawthorn tree. Now the lot was smooth with only the pump standing in the backyard. Daniel stopped for a moment. Tomorrow, he decided, he'd bring his father here. He'd show his father how that pump was begging for a house to go with it.

Daniel changed his clothes and when the service began, he was seated between Tillie and Jeremy at the back of the church where they could get away quickly after the benediction. It was not a good location for concentrating. Latecomers would enter and as the door opened, the spring day would burst in as if it were deliberately reminding folks indoors what they were missing. But finally even the last of the latecomers took their places. The door remained closed and Daniel tried to put his mind to the scripture. The Reverend Barnard was reading about Daniel and the lion's den. It was a story Daniel particularly liked and because his name was the same as the Daniel in the Bible, he thought he should be able to imagine what a person would do when he found himself in a lion's den. But it was beyond his power of imagining. He

235

couldn't even bring himself to think how he'd feel, let alone what he'd do. Instead Daniel studied Reverend Barnard and tried to picture him in a lion's den. He was a young man but so short and stocky, he didn't look young. He looked more like a round-faced, kindly uncle who'd feel out of place standing up to a lion anywhere.

While Reverend Barnard preached his sermon, Daniel looked about the church. There were said to be one hundred and one pews in the church, which he'd always thought was a strange number. Why wouldn't the person who had built the pews stop at a hundred? he wondered. He studied the people in the congregation, he thought about the sailing excursion, then when there was nothing else to think about, he began to count the pews, beginning at the front on the left aisle. He'd counted to forty-three when Reverend Barnard asked them to bow their heads in prayer.

Daniel leaned forward and closed his eyes. The room was hushed when the door opened behind him. It wasn't the careful opening of a latecomer and, indeed, at this time it could scarcely be a latecomer. The door suddenly crashed open and slammed shut. There was a heavy footstep and a voice broke right into the middle of Reverend Barnard's soft prayer.

"There's a regiment of British regulars marching here from Marblehead," the voice cried. "They're coming right through town. Headed for the North Bridge. For Robert Foster's."

Daniel spun around. Colonel David Mason was

standing at the back of the church, struggling for breath, his face red from running, his coat unbuttoned.

When Daniel turned back, the first thing he saw was Tom Carver leaping over the back of a pew. Colonel Pickering, who had only a few days ago received his promotion and been put at the head of the Essex Regiment, was striding down the center aisle and behind him, running on his short legs, was Reverend Barnard, his long, black preacher's robe hiked up around his knees. All over the church women and children were squeezing aside to let the men by. Jeremy was one of the first out. As he flung open the door to the pew, he called over his shoulder, "I'm going home for my gun. You two come along."

The troops were not yet in sight when Daniel and Tillie reached the front door, but all over town bells were ringing the alarm and outside, the scene was one of utter confusion. Women and children were scurrying in all directions; some men were untying horses from their hitching posts; others, along with Captain Mason, were running across the bridge to pull up the draw. Charlie and Benjie ran past toward the river. Colonel Pickering was already astride his horse, his face a torment of frustration. The Essex Regiment had had no practice, no preparation for assembling anywhere on a minute's notice, and all he could do was to go home for his own arms.

In the doorway a man from Marblehead, who had ridden into town with the news, was telling Reverend Barnard and others what he'd learned. He had posed as a Tory, it seemed, and talking to one of the soldiers in Marblehead, he'd found out that Paul Revere had suspected danger. He'd rowed out to Castle William, the island that General Gage had fortified in Boston Harbor, to investigate and he'd been captured. With him out of the way, the Sixty-Fourth Regiment of foot soldiers under Colonel Leslie had boarded a transport, the man said. They'd come to Marblehead but had kept out of sight until they knew everyone would be in church. Only then had they landed, counting on taking Salem by surprise, getting the cannon from Robert Foster's before there could be opposition.

Tillie picked up her skirts and with Daniel at her side she started home, setting as fast a pace as any man could. At the front door she scooped up Adams, her pet goose, and took him inside.

Jeremy was loading his musket.

"I'm going back with you, Jeremy," Daniel said.

Jeremy nodded, filling his pockets with cartridges. "Wish I had a gun."

"Hope no one needs one." Jeremy slung his musket over his shoulder. "I don't aim to use this unless I need to." He told Tillie to stay indoors and he and Daniel started off. "What I plan to do," Jeremy said, "is to station myself beside Tom Carver. We don't want any hotheads on our side, starting things off prematurely."

Daniel had to run to keep up with Jeremy. "How can you keep from firing?" he asked. "A whole armed regiment. You can't just push them away."

Jeremy didn't slacken his pace. "We can keep our wits about us, that's what we can do," he said. "Maybe we can outsmart the British. We've done it before."

Daniel thought of the two court sessions and the town meeting when they had, indeed, outsmarted the general, but this was a deliberate attack. Jeremy didn't seem to appreciate the difference, Daniel thought.

But if the situation seemed hopeless to Daniel then, it seemed even more hopeless when they arrived at the bridge. The troops were there now, halted before the drawn bridge, double lines of redcoats in perfect order, trained men, their bayonets glinting in the sun. In the midst of the regiment was a detachment with a cart, with pickaxes, with coils of rope, ready for the cannon they were so sure they would capture.

Daniel walked to the end of the bridge, near the wharf where the *Libera* was tied, not far from where Colonel Leslie was standing. He took his place beside Mr. Morris, the saddlemaker. When he looked back at the town now, it was not at the regiment but at the Salem forces. At the people who had gathered to oppose an empire. There was Colonel Pickering standing with an assortment of men in Sunday clothes, some of them with muskets, some of them without. There was the portly Reverend Barnard. Tom Carver was brandishing a gun and Jeremy was at his side. On the other side of the bridge where the draw was operated, David Mason stood, his coat still unbuttoned, and with him was Robert Foster holding a hammer. The few others were all unarmed and with the draw up, there was no way to get arms to them. Although there was a constant stream of men gathering, these were the men in the forefront. This was Salem's strength.

Daniel was only a few feet from Colonel Leslie. He watched the colonel pace back and forth. Then suddenly he stepped forward.

"I demand that the draw be lowered," he shouted. "What right have you to block the king's highway?"

For a moment there was no answer. Then someone on the other side called back. "This is no king's highway." The voice was leisurely. Insultingly leisurely. "This road belongs to the owners of lots on this side of the river. The king has nothing to do with it."

"We'll see about that!" the colonel shouted.

"If you know what's good for you," the voice drawled, "you'll leave the king out of this."

The colonel folded his arms across his chest. "I'll order my men to fire," he called.

The answer shot back. "Fire and be damned."

Daniel's heart pounded. He couldn't help but take pride in that voice across the river, standing up to the colonel against such odds, speaking out so bravely from such a pitiful position. But at the same time it seemed to Daniel that Salem was lost. The quotation from Sarah's sampler flashed into his mind. "Behold the day cometh." It cometh all right, Daniel thought. The day was here.

Colonel Leslie stood for a moment, considering the challenge. Then he came to attention. "I will fire," he said. He spun around to give the order but he found himself face to face not with the officer in charge but with the Reverend Barnard. He had been inching himself into position so that now he stood squarely between the colonel and his men, his short legs planted firmly apart.

"If you give the order to fire, it will be an act of war." He spoke in his pulpit voice that reached down the lines of the British soldiers. "We are unarmed citizens here, having come straight from church." Daniel glanced at the Salem men. Colonel Pickering was trying to look as dignified and martial as he could, but at Reverend Barnard's words, he quickly thrust his musket behind him. What other muskets there were disappeared too.

"If you fire," Reverend Barnard went on, "it cannot be regarded as an act of self-defense." He raised himself on his toes. "Are you ready," he asked, "to begin this conflagration at this spot at this moment? Do you, Colonel Leslie, wish to be the one who orders the first shot fired? Do you wish to stand before your Maker as the man who breaks the Sabbath in this way?"

Daniel let out his breath in a long sigh. The Reverend Barnard would do just fine in a lion's den. At the moment Colonel Leslie gave no order to fire. But neither did he give an order to retreat.

"My orders are to cross this bridge," he cried. "My orders are to get to the other side of the river. And I'll get to the other side if I have to wait forever to do it. I'll turn your warehouses into barracks—" he shouted but the rest of his words were lost. Salem was answering

241

back. From both sides of the river came the answer. "Stay and be welcome!" "Stay as long as you want!" "Stay till you freeze over for all we care!"

The saddlemaker leaned over to Daniel. "He's determined, that colonel. Wouldn't take many men to get control of the draw if they could just get a few of them across someway."

Colonel Leslie turned to the officers of the company standing near him. "Who do they think they are," he shouted, "blocking an army?" He went into consultation with the officers. The conversation was muted but occasionally a word would drift out from the group. Isolated words, they didn't mean much to Daniel, worried as he was by what the saddlemaker had said, studying the short distance that lay between the British troops and control of the draw. Then Colonel Leslie said one word that reached Daniel. The word was *boat*. Colonel Leslie was looking in the direction of the *Libera*.

Suddenly Daniel found himself running. No British soldier was going to take *his* boat to steal the cannon that belonged to *his* town. They weren't going to press the *Libera* into serving the British. Already he could hear footsteps pounding behind him on the wharf. Daniel flung himself into the boat and in one swift movement he had grabbed the ax from under the bow. A soldier was behind him. He ordered him to stop. Daniel paid no attention. He cut the line that tied the *Libera* to the wharf but before the boat could move off into the water, the soldier had jumped into the boat with him. The first thing the soldier would do would be to go for the paddles. Daniel leaned down and threw them overboard. When he straightened, his ax still in his hand, the soldier was standing before him, his bayonet pointed right at Daniel's stomach.

Behind the bayonet, the soldier was not even disconcerted. "That will be the end of your shenanigans," he said as though Daniel were only an irritation in the path of an army. "Drop that ax, Yankee," he said, "or I'll run you through. I may anyway." He joggled his bayonet at Daniel, so confident in its power that for a moment he didn't even bother to keep a firm grip on it. "Just who do you think you are, Yankee, to defy a British regular?"

Daniel's hand tightened on the ax. "I'm a Whig," he shouted. The word sounded so strong and sure, he repeated it. "A Whig! That's who I am! And I'll defy the whole British Empire if I want."

The man laughed. He was so assured with that uniform on and a bayonet in his hand that he glanced up at his friends on the dock to see if they appreciated the humor of a young boy in his Sunday clothes talking so big. He stood easy, his feet together, as if he were on dry land.

Daniel didn't plan what he was going to do. He suddenly raised his ax and swung it at the bayonet. He heard it clatter to the bottom of the boat and before the soldier could recover himself, Daniel rushed at the man, flinging his full weight at him, hurling himself against the soldier's knees, throwing him off balance in that easy stance of his, taking him by surprise, toppling him into the water. There was a splash and cheering from the shore. The boat had drifted away from the dock and was heading toward the bank. Daniel looked back at the dock. It was lined with redcoats. The river was lined with them and they weren't letting any Salem people near. Some of the soldiers were throwing a rope out to the man in the water. The rest of them were waiting for the *Libera* to continue its course to the shore, where in a few minutes they would take it.

Daniel raised his ax over his head. He brought it down on the bottom of the boat. The wood splintered and he raised his ax again. Tears were running down his face. "I'm sorry, mate," he said, "I'm sorry." Right between the ribs of the boat he crashed the ax, again and again, quickly, with all the strength of his body.

The water was coming through the hole now. It was lapping at Daniel's feet, covering his ankles. He glanced up. The *Libera* was drifting upstream with the incoming tide. It was listing to one side, lumbering toward the shore, but Daniel didn't drop his ax until he felt the *Libera* touch land. Then all he knew was that he was completely, thoroughly, painfully out of breath. His hands on the side of the *Libera*, his head lowered, his feet in the water, he worked for the next breath. At last his breathing was easier and Daniel looked up. He was farther from the bridge than he'd thought. And the soldiers on the shore were gone.

They'd apparently seen that the boat was unusable and they were back in formation. The saddlemaker was holding onto the boat.

And Jeremy was running up the bank. As Daniel stepped out of the boat, Jeremy put both arms around him. "You all right, boy?"

"I'm all right. What's happening?"

"You got your breath?"

"Yes."

"Then we'll go back and see what's happening." Jeremy pulled the *Libera* up on the shore. As they walked back to the bridge, he talked in jerks. An armed company from Danvers was on its way here now. To help Salem. There could be a full-scale battle. If Leslie didn't give in.

Daniel quickened his steps, although his shoes were so filled with water, it made walking difficult.

They were closer to the bridge now. Jeremy pointed at Colonel Pickering and Reverend Barnard, who were talking to Colonel Leslie, talking so earnestly that even from a distance one could feel the importance of their talk. "That's our only hope," Jeremy said. "Colonel Pickering has offered to strike a bargain."

"What kind of bargain?"

"He says Salem will lower the draw so that Colonel Leslie can carry out his orders. *If.*"

"If what?"

"If the British will march only thirty rods beyond the bridge and then turn about and march out of town."

"How far is Robert Foster's?"

"Forty-five rods."

"You think he'll do it?"

"I don't know. He's been told the Danvers men will be here soon."

Jeremy and Daniel stepped into the crowd of quiet onlookers, watching and waiting. Colonel Leslie stood with one knee thrust out, his face as determined as ever, while Colonel Pickering and Reverend Barnard talked. They didn't stop talking. When one left off, the other started.

The soldiers were at attention. On the other side of the bridge Colonel Mason, who knew about the bargain, stood with one hand on the wheel that would lower the draw.

Daniel studied Colonel Leslie's face. He had the same kind of stubborn, protruding jaw that Colonel Pickering himself had. Having stated so many times that he would cross the river, he would never retreat without crossing it. But would he retreat at all? And even if he agreed to Colonel Pickering's plan, could he be counted on to keep his word, a man who planned a surprise attack while folks were in church? Daniel couldn't detect a hint or a flicker in Colonel Leslie's face to betray what he was thinking. Then suddenly Leslie turned to Colonel Pickering and gave a curt nod.

Colonel Pickering stepped up to the bridge. "Colonel Mason," he called, "you can lower the draw!"

Once in a storm Daniel had watched men being

rescued from a ship sinking beyond the Neck. He had stood with the Salem onlookers and watched the rowboats go out to the ship, watched them disappear behind the waves, watched them make their way slowly back, out of sight for a moment, then back in sight, and during the whole proceedings not a word had been spoken on the Neck. Not until the last man was safe on shore did the quiet break. It was like that now. No one made a sound while the draw was lowered. The British troops started to march. They crossed the bridge. Ten rods. Fifteen. David Mason was standing at the thirty-rod mark and beyond him was Robert Foster's shop with the smoke drifting up from the chimney. People seemed to stop breathing as the troops approached David Mason. Only a few more feet now.

Then Colonel Leslie turned his head to one side. "Company!" he called. The word was picked up and thrown down the line. "Halt!" The long lines rippled and stopped.

"About face!"

Company by company the soldiers wheeled about. "Forward march!"

Back they marched, across the bridge, down the road to Marblehead, but not until the bridge was clear did Salem break loose with its cheers. Daniel tried to find his voice to add to the shouts of the onlookers but it wasn't there. He didn't feel like an onlooker. He felt more like one of the men rowing a rescue boat the day of the storm at the Neck; when they had reached safety, when the people on shore had cheered, those men hadn't said a word. They had only smiled. Daniel looked at Jeremy; he wasn't shouting either. He was grinning at Daniel and Daniel grinned back.

"It's over," Daniel said. "We sent them back, didn't we?"

"Yes, and without bloodshed. This time it was without bloodshed. Let's go home and tell Tillie."

It was Jeremy who told the news while Daniel sat in front of the fire, drying his feet. All he could think was that it was over. For a while it was hard to believe that what Jeremy was describing had actually taken place. Time didn't start again until there was a knock on Jeremy's door.

Suddenly the room was filled with people. Colonel Pickering was there and David Mason and the Reverend Barnard, his stiff preacher's collar wilted around his neck. They were smiling and taking chairs and Tillie was scurrying about pouring cider, and her goose, Adams, was walking from one to another, honking. Daniel took a chair too and the afternoon came back to life. It was as if all the rowers of the rescue boats were meeting after the storm and only as they talked could they appreciate how grave the storm had been. Indeed, only as they were together could they fully appreciate how sweet was the relief that it was over, how satisfying to have come through, and what warmth there was among them.

Colonel Pickering laughed. "And when Daniel told that soldier he was a Whig," he said, "you could have heard him all the way to Danvers!"

Daniel grinned. "Well, I didn't want there to be any mistake. I *am* a Whig. And proud of it."

All the celebrants had not arrived, however. In a moment the door burst open and Charlie and Benjie came in, all grins, all congratulations and excitement.

Charlie thumped Daniel on the back. "You see?" he said. "You see?" He turned to the others. "This is the fellow who asked me what a boy our age could do for Salem."

Daniel smiled. Up to now, he hadn't even thought about the fact that he'd been pressed.

More chairs were found, more cider poured, and then at the door there was still another knock. There was no bursting open of the door this time. The person outside waited while Tillie put down the cider jug, shooed Adams from under her feet, and went to the door to open it.

Dr. West walked into the room, leaning on a cane. His eyes went among the people as if he were dismissing them, one by one, and then they came to rest on Daniel.

"Are you all right, Daniel?" he asked.

Daniel stood before the hearth in his bare feet and it seemed to him that in that crowded room only he and his father were there.

"I'm fine," he said.

Dr. West's hat was still on his head, his attitude so intent, no one wanted to disturb him by even offering him a chair.

"I wasn't at the bridge," Dr. West said. "I couldn't

249

get anywhere near. But I heard what you did." He hesitated. "A person would have to feel strongly to do what you did." He hung his cane on the back of a chair. "It's been a long afternoon for me, Daniel. But your actions have made certain facts clear." He took a deep breath. "You've made the country's cause your cause. I can see that." He paused. "And I can't take you away from it." Slowly he reached into his pocket. "The only thing I can do is to stay with you." He pulled the big iron housekey out of his pocket and laid it on the kitchen table. "We'll start drawing up plans for a new house."

For a moment Daniel thought he was going to disgrace himself. He was afraid that standing before all those people, he might start to cry, but then Dr. West took off his hat and turned to Tillie with a smile. "Do you have another mug, Tillie?" he asked. "I could do with some cider."

The grown folks made a place at the table for Dr. West. There was fresh cider and doughnuts all around. Because there weren't enough chairs, Charlie and Benjie and Daniel squatted on the hearth with Adams at their feet.

Jeremy took his watch out from his vest pocket. "Four o'clock." He grinned. He raised his mug. "And all's well." He turned to Daniel. "What will we drink to, lad?" he asked.

The first toast was always drunk to the king.

Daniel hesitated. Then he stood up. "To the people," he said.

All the mugs were raised. Daniel looked around the

room. An outsider might not think the people were ready. But they were. There were storms ahead and missteps and setbacks, most likely, but they could weather them. They were ready. Even he was ready.

Author's Note

THE YEAR 1774 to 1775 was a momentous year not only for America as a whole but for individual Americans who had to decide once and for all whether they would put the British Empire or freedom first in their hearts. Most of them wanted both, but as the year progressed it became more and more apparent that they would have to put one before the other, and many loyal to the mother country came regretfully to the conclusion that if they wanted to preserve the right to govern themselves, they had to defy England, no matter what it might lead to. This is the story of the events that led one boy to switch his basic loyalties.

I have chosen to put this boy in Salem because as the temporary seat of the Massachusetts government, it was a center of high feeling and conflicting ideas which in turn led to almost more real drama than fiction can support. The story has been built around a backbone of real events beginning with Judge Ropes' death, including the two sessions of the General Court, the town meeting of August 24th, the fire of October 5th, and ending with the Affair at North Bridge on February 26th which was in reality, although no shots were fired, the first confrontation in the Revolutionary War. The course of that afternoon is related as close to the way it actually happened as I can determine, although, of course, Daniel and his boat were not there. Instead, there were three men, Joseph Whicher, Frank Benson and Hunter Felt, who scuttled their gondolas when it became apparent the British were going to use them. It is claimed in Salem history that Joseph Whicher was pricked by a British bayonet and so was the first American to shed blood in the war. It is also claimed that after Leslie's retreat Salem prepared a new rallying flag —a pure white bunting with a green pine on one side and an "appeal to heaven" on the other. In England the *Gentleman's Magazine* reported that the "Americans have hoisted their standard of liberty at Salem."

Two months later at the time of the battle of Lexington, John Pickering (Colonel Timothy's brother) wrote in his diary of husbandry: "April 19, 1775. Grafted on tree by pantry window . . . was grafting when I heard of Lexington Battle." Colonel Timothy Pickering, later to be Adjutant General under Washington and still later Secretary of War and then Secretary of State, was in his office at the Registry of Deeds when between eight and nine o'clock in the morning a rider informed him that the British troops had attacked the militia at Lexington. Colonel Pickering did not believe the troops from Salem could reach Lexington before the British returned to Boston but he mustered nearly three hundred men and began marching, halting in Danvers for a while on the expectation that he would hear the British troops had already returned. At the time, Colonel Pickering was severely criticized by some people who believed that if the Salem troops had taken quicker action they might have stopped the British at Charlestown, but in August the Provincial Congress vindicated the Salem companies by resolution.

After the Battle of Lexington, the Provincial Congress was anxious to report the news to England before General Gage could report it. Again Salem took a leading part. John Derby took the official dispatches on the *Quero* arriving in London on May 28, days ahead of General Gage's report on board the *Sukey*.

Daniel West and his family, Hannah, the Foote family, Benjie, Charlie, the two Thomases, Mr. Allison, Jeremy and Tillie are all fictional characters. Other Salem names such as David Mason, the Derbys, Peter Frye, Colonel Browne, the Pickerings, Robert Foster, Reverend Barnard, Judge Ropes, played a real part in Salem's history.

I am indebted to David R. Proper and other staff

members of the Essex Institute in Salem, to Philip Chadwick Foster Smith of the Peabody Museum, and to John Pickering who so kindly put his home and family papers at my disposal.

About the Author

This is JEAN FRITZ's eleventh book published by Coward-McCann, and it is the sort of book she particularly enjoys writing.

Mrs. Fritz was born in Hangkow, China, where her father was a missionary, and lived there until she was thirteen. She says, "I developed a deep homesickness that made me want to embrace not just a given part of America at a given time but the whole of it. I find my greatest pleasure in extending my own experience as an American back over the years, of trying to live in earlier periods as a contemporary of that period might."

Prerevolutionary Salem is a natural setting for the book, as Mrs. Fritz is "particularly intrigued with the periods of decision in our country when conflicting ideologies are at a point of tension and the individual has to make a choice." It is from these interests and ideas that her sensitive portrayal of Daniel and feeling for the period come.

Mrs. Fritz lives in Dobbs Ferry, New York, with her husband, Michael. They have two children.

About the Artist

LYND WARD is a noted illustrator of children's books. He is a Caldecott Medal winner, and his books have often been included in the "Fifty Books" selections of the American Institute of Graphic Arts. He lives in Cresskill, New Jersey.